Reasons for Learning

Expanding the Conversation on
Student-Teacher Collaboration

Reasons for Learning

Expanding the Conversation on Student–Teacher Collaboration

John G. Nicholls AND
Theresa A. Thorkildsen

EDITORS

FOREWORD BY SEYMOUR B. SARASON

Teachers College, Columbia University
New York and London

Published by Teachers College Press, 1234 Amsterdam Avenue, New York, NY 10027

Library of Congress Cataloging-in-Publication Data

Reasons for learning : expanding the conversation on student-teacher
  collaboration / edited by John G. Nicholls, Theresa A. Thorkildsen.
     p.   cm.
  Includes bibliographical references and index.
  ISBN 0-8077-3398-9 (alk. papers).—ISBN 0-8077-3397-0 (pbk. :
  alk. papers)
    1. Motivation in education.   2. Interaction analysis in education.
  3. Teacher-student relationships.   4. Classroom management.
  I. Nicholls, John G.   II. Thorkildsen, Theresa A.
  LB1065.R384   1995
  370.1'54—dc20   94-24120

ISBN 0-8077-3397-0 (paper)
ISBN 0-8077-3398-9 (cloth)

Printed on acid-free paper
Manufactured in the United States of America

01 00 99 98 97 96 95 8 7 6 5 4 3 2 1

Dedication

Love and work was a caption that John and I, as husband and wife, privately used to stimulate our imaginations and urge ourselves to creative thought. Although he had his professional work and I had mine, we always designated at least one project *our* work. This book is the final product of that commitment. John G. Nicholls died on September 29, 1994 at the age of 54. The contributors and I would like to dedicate this book to John, who taught us to become less "divided against ourselves" and to seek "conjoint communicated experiences" wherein we combine love and work.

Theresa A. Thorkildsen

It is . . . a sound instinct which identifies freedom with power to frame
purposes and to . . . carry into effect purposes so framed.

–John Dewey

Those who hate gardening need a theory. Not to garden without a theory is a
shallow, unworthy way of life.

A theory must be convincing and scientific. Yet to various people,
various theories are convincing and scientific. Therefore, we need a number
of theories.

The alternative to not-gardening without a theory is to garden. However,
it is much easier to have a theory than actually to garden.

–Leszek Kolakowski

Science-making that is . . . based on different values than those prevailing in
the culture at a given time, and thus attempts to discover, explore, and
explain different realities, tends to be ignored–or attacked as "unscientific."
This judgment can frequently be understood for what it really is . . . a charge
of heresy.

–Barbara Du Bois

Contents

Foreword

I had three very strong reactions to this book. The first was one of poignant regret that it was not available when I wrote *The Failure of Educational Reform* (1991), *Letters to a Serious Education President* (1993), and *The Case for Change: Rethinking the Preparation of Educators* (1993). If it had been available, I would have had more compelling evidence for what I was saying. Compelling is an appropriate adjective. It is not that this book emphasizes points others have not made earlier but rather that these points are made with such candor, clarity, detail, and balance as to be truly gripping. Put another way, unlike almost every comparable edited book, this one has a cumulative effect. Anyone unfamiliar with the phenomenology of teachers—and a diverse assortment at that—is in for an instructive, effective, and intellectual experience. And for those who are in the game at any level of the educational hierarchy, reading this book will remind them of several things. First, teaching is a taxing, frustrating, satisfying, mind-bending, and mind-altering role for those who have not fallen prey to apathy and routine, even though many of the contributors to this book were in contexts where apathy or passivity would have been understandable.

Second, unless the teacher starts with a clear and realistic understanding of what students are and where they are coming from—what I have called the big but simple idea—they are doomed to feel inadequate and impotent, too frequently explaining their plight in the spirit of the dynamics of blaming the victim. Not every teacher who contributed to this book started with such an understanding, but they came to such an understanding before it was too late, gaining the courage from somewhere to see that *they* had to change if their students were to change.

Third, it is obvious that the formal preparation of these individuals for the realities of classrooms and schools was, to indulge understatement, inadequate and misleading. This point is of enormous significance because it exposes the major limitations of almost all efforts at educational reform: They are efforts at repair, not prevention. We have been addicted to the repair effort, even though in an abstract way we know that prevention is incomparably more effective (and less costly) than repair efforts, which at best can claim very modest results and too frequently can claim no positive results at all. Given the ills of our educational system it is, I suppose, understandable that the pressures to do something are impossible to ignore. But it is one thing wholly to cave in to such pressures and quite another thing to seek a balance between repair and prevention. To understand all is not to forgive all.

The power this book gives implicitly and explicitly to the importance of prevention was the nexus of my second strong reaction. Let me state it in more concrete terms. If after reading this book the reader were to ask How many of the "lessons" contained in this book are the basis for organizing, suffusing, and implementing preparatory programs for educators—not only teachers but administrators as well—the answer, as John Goodlad and I have argued, varies from nothing to little. I am sure there are exceptions; there always are. But they are exceptions. The contents of this book should, I would hope, cause the reader seriously to reflect on the question as well as his or her answer. How many sleep-producing task force reports say we need "better trained teachers"? All of them genuflect before the obvious. How many of these rhetorical barbiturates give any recognition to the experiences and conclusions so beautifully presented in this book? None, to my knowledge. I have read most of these insomnia-curing reports. Again I have to say that there probably are exceptions. But I say that not out of conviction but from respect for the impersonal laws of probability.

The third of my strong reactions to this book concerns the point that unless the external pressures for change (i.e., coming from critics and policymakers "out there") do not cause the educational community to engage in honest self-scrutiny, to assume the responsibility for intellectual, substantive, provocative leadership, to own up to Pogo's "we have met the enemy and it is us," to eschew clichés and empty generalities, to recognize that salvation comes from within and not from without—unless these begin to happen, no improvement can be expected.

Rarely have I read a book that contains so much serious, productive soul searching. There is a maxim among psychotherapists that a person's decision to seek help means that the person is halfway on the road to desired change. To accept responsibility, at least to a significant degree, is the essential first step. That, I hasten to say, does not mean that external, contextual factors are not powerful, constraining, and upsetting. To downplay such factors would be worse than nonsense. It would be wrong, stupid, and immoral. But it does mean that you have to take responsibility for your contribution to your plight.

No one willed the present ills in our schools. There are no villains.

Nothing I have said was intended as *ad hominem*, which, unfortunately and frequently, external critics of our schools explicitly intend. It is far easier to deal with villains than with well-intentioned educators imprisoned in tradition and by orientations that render self-scrutiny extraordinarily difficult. I know whereof I speak. It took me years to unlearn the conventional wisdom, to be hit over the head enough times so as to force me to face the sources of my failures. So, for example, there was a time when I truly believed that dramatically increasing expenditures for education would discernibly increase quality. Giving up that belief was not easy, nor was it easy to say so in writing. I am not in favor of malign neglect. I am quite aware that there are schools the physical conditions of which are so abysmal, and their lack of even minimally acceptable resources so glaring, as to be morally inexcusable. On a MacNeil-Lehrer Newshour program aired on February 8, 1993, there was a segment on a midwestern school system that, under the jurisdiction of the courts, was required to spend $1 billion for new buildings and new programs and resources. Visually the results are stunning. In terms of educational and social outcomes the program ends on a dispiriting note. If money cannot buy you happiness, it also cannot buy you the educational outcomes you seek. Indeed, one of the momentous and encouraging changes in the beliefs of many educators over the past two decades is having had to give up the belief that there is no major educational problem that money cannot dramatically alter in desirable ways. Unfortunately, this change in belief has not emboldened educational leaders to state their change of view publicly. Unlike the contributors to this book, their self-scrutiny remains private, unusable, and a reinforcer of the status quo. I used to say about reform efforts that the more things change, the more they remain the same. I now think otherwise: The more things remain as they are, as long as we continue to think as we do, the situation will get worse. I can assure the reader that having predicted the current state of affairs, and now predicting that things will get worse, is no cause for personal satisfaction. But I can assure those who will read this book that they will be provided a basis for hope because its implicit and explicit messages point us in the direction we have to go.

Seymour B. Sarason
Yale University

John G. Nicholls and Theresa A. Thorkildsen

Introduction

BEYOND WHAT WORKS

John G. Nicholls and Theresa A. Thorkildsen

Widening the Conversation on Motivation in Education was our original title for this book, but the term *motivation* came to seem too narrow. Motivation in education has tended to be the specialty of psychologists with a penchant for abstract theory and technical approaches to change. They have sought to promote motivation by finding ways to convince students they *can* or *should* do whatever someone else has already declared important. Too much writing reflects a football-coach metaphor, wherein the problem is how to motivate the team to get the ball into the end zone. There is no place in that vision for ethical, political questions such as whether there should be an end zone or how many end zones we might construct and which if any we should favor.

In this volume we attend to the question of what teachers and students believe they should be working toward, or what they see as legitimate reasons for learning. We work toward the idea of teachers and students as moral agents whose involvements and accomplishments reflect their evaluation of the appropriateness of the options, or lack of options, open to them. There is a rising interest in teacher voice and teacher lore, which does cast teachers as moral agents. But this rarely extends to students. In *A Theory of Justice*, John Rawls (1971) argues that social justice demands that individuals be permitted to realize and exercise their competencies. Yet students are almost never asked about the fairness of the attempts teachers make to influence their competencies, or of the ways they and their classmates treat one another in school.

So one of the themes of this book is that studies of student engagement in learning are, and should be seen as, moral inquiries about what better schools might look like: inquiries about what students' and teachers' reasons for learning should be, and what sorts of lives should be constructed in school.

A second, associated theme is that those people most intimately involved in the daily work of education should also be most intimately

1

engaged in this moral inquiry. They should not be cast merely as the receivers of theoretical principles or empirical generalizations about how to make schools that work to ends they have had no part in forming. A widened conversation is needed if schooling is to be more than a dull preparation for a predetermined future life—if it is to become, as Dewey wanted, a vigorous part of life in progress.

A symposium at a recent meeting of the American Educational Research Association concerned collaboration among teachers and academics in research on motivation. Among the speakers was a public school teacher who had been collaborating with researchers from a prestigious university. She said how valuable the experience had been and observed that the collaboration had enabled her to meet some "very important people." She meant prestigious professors. This book expresses our doubt that professors are more important than teachers or that teachers are more important than students in the negotiation of the reasons for learning, and directions of lives in schools. It is, in part, an answer to those very different teachers in our university classes who, though willing to listen to professors, ask for more writing by and with teachers. In the future, we hope these teachers will ask that student voices also be heard.

Seeing teachers and students as researchers has, in the past, meant obliging them to read and speak the language of the psychological journal, the laboratory, or abstract social theory. As the first chapter of this book suggests, such language can lead its devotees astray. Too often, learning to become a researcher means learning not to think or experience school as would exemplary teachers. Something is wrong if we do not have legitimate and popular forms of research and writing that, in and of themselves, move researchers closer to the concerns of those who seek to improve their teaching and communicate more robustly and sensitively with students.

For these reasons the tone of this book is, like teaching, personal and particular, not impersonal, abstract, and general. Generalizations and overarching, abstract theories can help us see particularities we might otherwise miss. But no teacher faces the representative class that some researchers love to describe. The exaltation of the general and the abstract over the particular can undermine those most intimately engaged in education. It can take us away from concern for particular people. Without particular people there might be grand ideas, but there can be no education. The bottom line is whether the present experience of particular students and teachers is educative.

It is one thing to say that research is not responsive to the needs of teachers and students. It is quite another to offer concrete alternatives. We did not wish to contribute more abstract language calling for greater responsiveness. Could we learn to care about particular people only by studying abstract theses about the importance of care? Could teaching become research if teachers read only abstract theses about teaching as research? We present particular stories. Like friends in conversation, we hope to provoke others to tell contrary and converging stories.

This might sound easy, but the new educational omelet cannot be made without breaking eggs. Educational reform is students, teachers, and researchers making new moral choices and living new lives. This is not sweet and easy, but it can be exciting.

OVERVIEW

The first chapter involves an examination of teachers' and student teachers' evaluations of certain practices that would influence student motivation. It is commonly assumed that teachers are unaware of the generalizations researchers would offer them about how to foster a love of learning. Researchers, however, have not tested this assumption of teacher ignorance. When it is examined, the assumption is found wanting. Teachers, nevertheless, often do not teach so as to foster a love of learning—they do not do the things they believe will increase student motivation. This puzzle appears to reflect the fact that love of learning falls relatively low in the priorities of most schools and classrooms. The implication is that changing schooling might require us to change what we are trying to accomplish, rather than simply what we know about student engagement in learning.

In Chapter 2, a similar conclusion emerges in a totally different way. What began as an attempt by teachers and an administrator to conduct a traditional experiment turned out to be an ethical inquiry in which teachers developed new purposes for teaching. They critiqued their curricula, evolved new reasons for teaching, and found themselves listening more closely to their students. When working on the project, the participants were not fully conscious that they were engaged in an ethical inquiry. One suggestion that emerges is that educational inquiry might be conducted more adequately if it were named ethical inquiry from the outset.

In Chapter 3, a study of the writing of Sylvia Ashton-Warner, the focus on students is more marked. When teaching and writing about her experiences, Ashton-Warner struggles to reconstruct her own reasons for teaching and the visions of life she wants in her classroom. The transformation in teaching she describes involves connecting school experience to students' most powerful and intimate personal experiences. Writing about all this is an essential part of Ashton-Warner's teaching, researching, and personal-professional growth.

In Chapter 4, a high school teacher records and reflects on his own personal and intellectual transformation. This begins when he is prodded by rebellious students, and research findings he initially abhors, to begin the sort of listening to students that Ashton-Warner describes. Giving up old ways proves difficult, but reveals new satisfactions—new reasons for teaching.

In the remaining chapters, student voices become still more important. Action research has tended to present the teacher as a solitary reflective inquirer. The last three chapters can be seen as examples of action research in which students and teachers become collaborators in inquiries about the means and ends of schooling.

In Chapter 5, a principal and a teacher ask their low-income, African-American students direct questions about their mathematics curriculum. Students objected to this traditional curriculum, yet they also resisted the change their teacher proposed. In the end, many students are converted to a new approach and their teacher becomes an advocate of more democratic education.

In the last two chapters, students are involved directly in the negotiation of the shape of life in school. They are not merely asked to choose topics or methods, but provoked to articulate the reasons for their preferences. In Chapter 6, second-grade students debate the nature of science. Most of them see science as the exploration of the unknown. At variance with many science curricula that emphasize noncontroversial knowledge, they favor the unknown. Their intellectual adventures exemplify the notion that science should teach tolerance.

In Chapter 7, fourth- and fifth-graders face the question of how their learning groups should be chosen. Researchers' recommendations create problems for these students. The project highlights the danger of insensitivity to local people and conditions, and the problems of promoting, in the name of science, single answers to inherently controversial questions. Encouraging students to speak on such questions might make them more able and committed to forming, in concert with others, sound reasons for learning.

1 Big Science, Little Teachers

KNOWLEDGE AND MOTIVES CONCERNING STUDENT MOTIVATION

John G. Nicholls, University of Illinois at Chicago
Susan B. Nolen, University of Washington

Give them some say in the ...

Give them some choice in, for example, which book they will read ...
they will attempt.

Say, "You were very good today" if they start to improve.

4. Tell them, when they try hard, "You are a good boy/girl."

15. Tell them, "Good boy/girl" when they start on their work.

16. Tell them, "I like the way you are paying attention" when they do this.

17. When they do poorly, say, "That's because you didn't try hard."

Motivation questionnaire

Teachers' and student teachers' common sense on motivation is often given little credence by researchers, and teachers often reciprocate by questioning the relevance of research. This chapter reports an attempt to check whether common sense on motivation is as primitive as academic researchers often assume. The results suggest that a lack of knowledge about student motivation on the part of teachers might not be the main reason for the fact that there is little love of learning in most schools.

Big Science. Hallelujah. Big Science. Yodellayheehoo.

—Laurie Anderson

According to one professor, the properly schooled student of psychology will believe that "you can never be certain of your facts in psychology unless you have research to back them up," and that "intuition and personal experience are [not] important sources of proof for psychological facts" (Friedrich, 1990, p. 25). Researchers seem to have parallel views about teachers' and student teachers' commonsense notions about student motivation. They write articles and books with titles like, "What teachers need to know" (Ames, 1990), "From theory to practice" (Stipek, 1988), and "A theory and its implications" (Nicholls, 1983). The researchers, it would seem, assume they have something worthwhile to tell teachers and not much to learn from them. The assumption that teachers are poorly informed about motivation has, however, not been subject to inquiry. Belatedly wanting to be good researchers—and not rely only on our intuitions—we thought we should begin to check. If you are a teacher or a student teacher, and unfamiliar with the academic research on student motivation, is your common sense likely to be at odds with what researchers would want to tell you?

COMMON SENSE

What then is common sense, or ordinary knowledge? Common sense is deceptive. It is, says Clifford Geertz (1983), "a relatively organized body of considered thought, rather than just what anyone clothed in his right mind knows" (p. 75). Yet "it is an inherent characteristic of common-sense thought to deny this and to affirm that its tenets are immediate deliverances of experience, not deliberated reflections upon it. . . . Religion rests its case on revelation, science on method . . . but common sense rests its on the assertion that it is not a case at all, just life in a nutshell" (p. 75).

Geertz would have us see common sense as a sophisticated, culturally constructed, worked-out body of thought. In this respect, scientific thought and common sense are similar, but how do they differ? Geertz (1983) uses one of Wittgenstein's metaphors. "Our language can be seen as an old city: a maze of little streets and squares, of old and new houses, and of houses with additions from various periods; and this surrounded by a multitude of modern sections with straight regular streets and uniform houses" (p. 73). The old city represents colloquial culture and the newer additions the more consciously organized culture of contemporary science.

Some citizens of cities hope that the new and the old will coexist fruitfully. Others hope that one will triumph over the other. It is similar in educational thought. Some resist the new, some resist the old, and others have diverse visions of constructive exchange between the two. In this chapter, our initial question was about the level of convergence between common sense and researchers' generalizations about student motivation. After we answer this question, we consider what the relationship between the two should be.

COMMON BELIEFS ABOUT STUDENT MOTIVATION

To estimate whether teachers and student teachers know what researchers would tell them, we devised a questionnaire (Nolen & Nicholls, 1994). Its important feature is that it includes a range of strategies for influencing motivation—from some that are strongly approved by many researchers to others that are not approved. This questionnaire is shown in Figure 1.1. We suggest that you answer it before reading on. (Students in our classes have found the items interesting as starters for discussion of motivation.)

You might find the questionnaire slightly frustrating to answer without more details about an actual student. But most advice given by researchers also has this generic quality. Whether writing for one another or for teachers, psychological researchers usually seek to generalize—to make statements that are true on the average. They do not usually focus on particular cases (Robinson, 1993). Thus, to make a reasonably direct comparison of researchers' views with those of teachers, we developed a collection of generalizations and formed them into this questionnaire.[1]

The average answers of a sample of 178 teachers and a sample of 276 student teachers are shown in Table 1.1. The items are grouped into sections on the basis of factor analysis of the teachers' and student teachers' answers. This method groups together items that have similar meanings. It provides a check that items we thought were similar in meaning also looked similar to the teachers and student teachers.

The groups of items in Table 1.1 are ranked from most to least favored by teachers and student teachers. There is appreciable research supporting this ranking (Nolen & Nicholls, 1994). Our reading of the research evidence (and our common sense) indicates that intrinsic motivation for learning is enhanced by attributing interest to students, promoting student collaboration, and giving students some choice of tasks and approaches to their work. These strategies were rated highly by the teachers and student teachers. Emphasizing competition and comparison among

FIGURE 1.1. Survey of Beliefs About the Effectiveness of Strategies for Influencing Motivation

Directions: You are teaching a class (at the grade level you normally teach) that has a few children who lack all interest in learning. They are not at all disruptive. But they daydream, are slow to start assignments, do not work hard, and are falling further and further behind the other students. Below are some possible things you could say or do to improve the motivation of such students. Indicate how useful you think each thing would probably be for improving the motivation of these students.

Answers: 1. Very harmful   2. Somewhat harmful   3. Neutral
4. Somewhat useful   5.Very useful

Tell them when they try hard, "You are a good boy (or girl)."	1 2 3 4 5
Tell them "Good boy/girl when they start on their work."	1 2 3 4 5
Say "You were very good today," if they start to improve.	1 2 3 4 5
Tell them "You will have trouble in higher grades if you don't work hard in this class."	1 2 3 4 5
Tell them "You will have to do better if you're going to get a good job when you leave school."	1 2 3 4 5
Say "You'll get further and further behind if you don't try harder."	1 2 3 4 5
Tell them "You could be one of the best students if you tried harder."	1 2 3 4 5
Say "If you try harder, you will do better."	1 2 3 4 5
When they do poorly, say, "That's because you didn't try hard."	1 2 3 4 5
Make them complete assignments in periods when other students are allowed free choice.	1 2 3 4 5
Keep them behind at recess when they don't complete assignments and only release them when they do.	1 2 3 4 5

students and providing extrinsic rewards for participation have been found not to have positive effects. Teachers and student teachers also gave these practices low ratings.

Overall, then, the teachers and student teachers knew pretty much what the research psychologists would want to tell them about increasing intrinsic motivation to learn. There were only slight differences between teachers and student teachers—suggesting that our questionnaire indeed tapped common sense rather than the specific fruits of teaching experience.

Even though we, the authors of this chapter, have both qualified and practiced as public school teachers, we started out ready to believe that teachers and student teachers might need enlightenment from people who have been initiated into the mysteries of research. Our excuse for not anticipating our findings is that we knew in advance that

FIGURE 1.1. (*Continued*)

Find what they really like, such as pizza or comic books, and offer them a reward for improvement.	1 2 3 4 5
Tell them they can have a treat if they work hard all day (or week depending on the severity of the problem).	1 2 3 4 5
Tell them you'll give them 50¢ every time they score above the class average on a test.	1 2 3 4 5
Tell them "Your best is good enough for me and it should be for you."	1 2 3 4 5
Say "It's fine not to hurry; just try to understand the work you do finish."	1 2 3 4 5
Tell them it's okay if they don't finish a project, as long as they try.	1 2 3 4 5
Put them in cooperative learning groups.	1 2 3 4 5
Sit them with someone who will help them learn.	1 2 3 4 5
Have them choose a project to do with another student.	1 2 3 4 5
Give them some say in the way they write up their work.	1 2 3 4 5
Give them some choice in, for example, which book they will read or which math problem they will attempt.	1 2 3 4 5
Allow them a bit of choice in the order in which they do their assignments.	1 2 3 4 5
Find interesting problems that will puzzle them.	1 2 3 4 5
Give them tasks that will stimulate them to think in new ways.	1 2 3 4 5
Look for opportunities to let them have class responsibilities.	1 2 3 4 5
Show a real interest in their hobbies or other interests.	1 2 3 4 5
Find ways to let them lead activities.	1 2 3 4 5
Occasionally say "I can see you are really thinking about this subject" when they show a bit of interest in their work.	1 2 3 4 5
Tell them when they are paying some attention to their work, "You really have been thinking about this."	1 2 3 4 5
Tell them "You are really improving" when they show some interest.	1 2 3 4 5

the practices the teachers and student teachers rated most highly are not often seen in the schools (Goodlad, 1984; Newby, 1991). Teachers don't commonly do the things they rate as most likely to enhance motivation.

Our initial reaction to our computer printout was, therefore, to suspect that we had inadvertently reversed our answer scale so that 1 instead of 5 meant endorsement of a strategy. But this was not so. Our results, which held up with different groups, induced us to face it: When asked to consider a collection of strategies, without the benefit of the information available to researchers on the effects of these strategies, teachers and student teachers rank them pretty much as researchers would. This does not mean teachers and student teachers have nothing to learn. It does mean, we believe, that researchers need to question their common sense about what student teachers and teachers know.

TABLE 1.1. Clusters of Strategies for Enhancing Motivation

Strategies	Average answers	
	Teachers	Student Teachers
Show Interest and Give Responsibility	4.67	4.68
Look for opportunities to let them have class responsibilities.		
Show a real interest in their hobbies or other interests.		
Find ways to let them lead activities.		
Attribute Thought and Improvement	4.45	4.49
Occasionally say, "I can see you are really thinking about		
this subject" when they show a bit of interest in their work.		
Tell them, when they are paying some attention to their work,		
"You really have been thinking about this."		
Tell them, "You are really improving" when they show some interest.		
Promote Cooperation	4.44	4.39
Put them in cooperative learning groups.		
Sit them with someone who will help them learn.		
Have them choose a project to do with another student.		
Select Stimulating Tasks	4.21	4.16
Find interesting problems that will puzzle them.		
Give them tasks that will stimulate them to think in new ways.		
Give Choice	4.21	4.06
Give them some say in the way they write up their work.		
Give them some choice in, for example, which book they will read		
or which math problem they will attempt.		
Allow them a bit of choice in the order in which they do		
their assignments.		
Encourage Progress	3.31	3.45
Tell them, "Your best is good enough for me and it should be for you."		
Say, "It's fine not to hurry; just try to understand the work you do finish."		
Tell them it's OK if they don't finish a project as long as they try.		

Not everyone agrees. One anonymous researcher who reviewed the fuller report of this study (Nolen & Nicholls, 1994), did not accept our findings. This person wrote, "[When I ask for] their definition of motivation and what they would do to facilitate student motivation . . . I am constantly amazed by my preservice teachers' lack of insight about student motivation." The reviewer appealed to his or her own teaching experience to dismiss both our research and the idea that the experience of teachers and student teachers teaches them anything of value.

All we can say is that the experience of conducting this research made us think again, and wonder (among other things) why researchers' recommendations were more similar to teachers' and student teachers'

TABLE 1.1. (*Continued*)

Strategies	Average answers	
	Teachers	Student Teachers
Praise	3.20	3.22
Tell them, when they try hard, "You are a good boy (or girl)."		
Tell them, "Good boy/girl when they start on their work."		
Say, "You were very good today," if they start to improve.		
Demand Completion of Assignments	3.15	2.92
Make them complete assignments in periods when other students are allowed free choice.		
Keep them behind at recess when they don't complete assignments and only release them when they do.		
Use Task-extrinsic Rewards	3.10	3.16
Find what they really like, such as pizza or comic books, and offer them a reward for improvement.		
Tell them they can have a treat if they work hard all day (or week depending on the severity of the problem).		
Tell them you'll give them 50¢ every time they score above the class average on a test.		
Attribute Failure to Low Effort	2.30	2.28
Tell them, "You will have trouble in higher grades if you don't work hard in this class."		
Tell them, "You will have to do better if you're going to get a good job when you leave school."		
Say, "You'll get further and further behind if you don't try harder."		
Tell them, "You could be one of the best students if you tried harder."		
Say, "If you try harder, you will do better."		
When they do poorly, say, "That's because you didn't try hard."		

Answers: 1. Very Harmful   2. Somewhat Harmful   3. Neutral   4. Somewhat Useful   5. Very Useful
Mean Answers by Teachers ($n = 178$) and Student Teachers ($n = 276$)

views than we expected them to be. Perhaps researchers have spread their words so widely that anyone coming into teaching knows these things? On the other hand, it could be that researchers have what wisdom they do because they avoid straying too far from the common wisdom that has accrued in our culture. Presumably there is some truth in both positions. Researchers are part of the stream of common culture and, like common people, receive from as well as contribute to it.

In any event, the general convergence of common sense and research-based views is our first major finding. We take it to mean that teachers and students should not toss out their common sense when researchers start speaking. But there is a second finding.

BIG SCIENCE AND LITTLE TEACHERS AT ODDS

Our other important finding involved a type of strategy that the teachers and student teachers rejected, but that many researchers have advocated. This strategy involved telling a student who had performed or learned poorly that he or she has not done well "because you didn't try hard," and that "if you try harder, you will do better." These statements clustered with "You will have trouble in the higher grades if you don't work hard in this class," "You'll get further and further behind if you don't try harder," and "You will have to do better if you are going to get a good job when you leave school."

The teachers and student teachers saw this cluster of statements as the least effective of the nine clusters. (See Table 1.1.) Yet one of the most popular methods proposed by psychological researchers and text writers involves telling students who feel personally defeated by schoolwork that the reason for their failure is their lack of effort.[2] In other words, the strategy on which researchers and teachers are at odds is one that many researchers (but not all) have publicly favored. This makes it an interesting case to examine further. Two questions arise: First, do researchers or teachers have a better reading of the value of this strategy and, second, what might account for the discrepancy?

BIG SCIENCE ADRIFT

We had doubts about the value of telling students their failures are due to low effort. This was, in part, because of a flaw in the original study allegedly supporting the notion of telling students that their difficulties reflect a lack of effort. This study (Dweck, 1975) was a comparison of two treatments, one of which led students to persist more in the face of failure. But because the two treatments differed in two aspects, it is not possible to be sure what accounts for the beneficial effect. The first treatment involved a mixture of easy and difficult tasks, so that students failed some tasks and succeeded on others. When the students in this condition failed, they were told, "That means you should have tried harder" (Dweck, 1975, p. 679). The second condition differed from the first in that students were *not* offered explanations for their outcomes *and* encountered a series of easy tasks on which they always succeeded. The greater persistence of students in the first condition could have resulted from the mixture of successes and failures they experienced and have nothing to do with what students were told. In the language of behaviorism, an intermittent reinforcement schedule—successes and failures—

produces greater resistance to extinction—more persistence in the face of failure—than a continuous schedule of easy successes.

Another reason for doubting the value of attributing students' failures to low effort appeared in the same year in the same research journal as Dweck's attributional retraining study. This study compared the effect of telling students they *should try* harder with the effects of telling them they *are trying* hard (Miller, Brickman, & Bolen, 1975). Telling students they are trying hard produced a considerable increase in performance, whereas telling them they need to try harder did not. A subsequent study also clearly supported this conclusion (Schunk, 1982). These studies suggest it is inadvisable to say such things as "You should try harder" or "You are not trying hard." This is telling students they are lazy—that they *don't* work hard. It is labeling negative behavior rather than fostering something constructive. These studies suggest it is better to find occasions when it is plausible to say students *are* doing what we hope they will do, better to tell students that they *are* trying hard or trying to make sense. This conclusion, emerging from the studies of Miller et al. and Schunk, is in line with the beliefs of teachers. They saw it as effective to tell students (when they pay some attention to schoolwork) such things as, "You really have been thinking about this."

But the message of Miller et al. (1975) and Schunk (1982) was barely heard by researchers. For example, Försterling (1985) reviewed the research on methods of improving motivation. He concluded that "attributional retraining methods have been consistently successful . . . attributional retraining consists primarily of teaching participants that their failures are due to lack of effort" (p. 509). But Försterling's conclusion does not follow from the research he reviewed. The studies he reviewed involved other things besides attribution of failure to low effort. Some involved telling students that their successes reflect high effort and that their failures reflect low effort. Others involved telling students only that they were hard workers—a strategy the teachers and student teachers favored. Furthermore, Försterling overlooked the evidence (Miller et al., 1975; Schunk, 1982) that attributing low effort to students does not increase persistence or achievement.

On this occasion, many scientists got themselves lost, whereas teachers and student teachers did not. The study many researchers relied on does not support its claim well. Nor do others. Furthermore, other studies suggest that the strategy of telling students that their failures reflect low effort is of no value. For some reason, the original notion that it helps to tell students that their failures reflect their lack of effort did not become quickly reconstructed.

LOST ON THE FRONTIER OF SCIENCE

How can this have come about? Mistakes are routine, but researchers should check and refine the ideas of their predecessors. The interesting question is not how the original mistake occurred but why it was not rectified. Why, when the idea is at odds with common sense and the evidence, did not more researchers question it? Perhaps it is because the idea was delivered in abstract scientistic language—a language that does not invite you to imagine what it would feel like to have someone tell you, "The reason you are doing poorly is that you have not been trying hard."

This language is that of attribution theory (Weiner, 1979). This approach to motivation started with the assumption that it is important to study people's commonsense explanations for events. Though common sense became the object of study, the language used to analyze it was far from everyday talk. Attribution theorists constructed a sort of universal periodic table to categorize people's explanations for events such as getting a grade of A or of F. They speak of the factors that produce success or failure in terms of whether they are stable or unstable, internal or external, and controllable or uncontrollable. These researchers seek to decide how to categorize assertions such as, "My report card looks bad because the teacher hates me." Is the causal factor accounting for the poor report card stable? (That is, does the student see this as something that will stay the same?) Is it controllable? (Can the student change it?) Is it an internal factor? (Is it a characteristic of the student versus something in the environment?)

A popular view among attribution theorists is that a lack of motivation can result when students attribute their failures to a stable, internal, uncontrollable factor. If, the argument goes, I attribute my failures to a more or less permanent characteristic of me, I have little reason to think I will be able to reverse my fortunes in the future. I will see little point in trying to improve. On the other hand, students who attribute failure to an internal, unstable, controllable factor have within their grasp the means of preventing future failure. This is reasonable and, reasonably enough, there is research evidence to support it (Weiner, 1979).

The next step is the question of how to improve the motivation of the student who attributes failure to an internal, stable, uncontrollable factor. The answer, in the same language, is to suggest to this student that the failure is better attributed to an internal, unstable, controllable factor. This sounds very reasonable as long as one sticks to the jargon of attribution theory. But forget that jargon and think what it means when translated into common language. You are a child who has repeatedly failed at mathematics and finally given up, believing yourself to be incompetent. To have a teacher tell you, when you fail yet again, "That means you should have tried harder" might be close to, "You sure are lazy." Thus, teachers and student teachers putting themselves in the shoes of students appear to see things that psychologists wielding abstract terms like *internal*, *controllable*, and *unstable* do not.[3]

Psychologists are not the only ones who can be bewitched by this abstract jargon. Giving a talk on motivation to a group of teachers, one of us (John Nicholls) asked them what they thought about the idea that, when students who have lost hope of success in school fail, one should say that it is because they didn't try hard enough. The group quickly rejected this strategy, noting its negative nature and the fact that it labels students as lazy. Like those who answered our questionnaire, they favored attributing positive qualities to students. At the end of the session, however, the teachers' supervisor wanted John to say more about the literature on attribution retraining. The supervisor used the attribution theory jargon, referring to the strategy of attributing failures to an internal, unstable factor. John reminded her that (without using the jargon) he had asked the teachers what they thought of this strategy and that they had quickly rejected it. He reiterated their reasons and said that he agreed with them. The supervisor repeated the jargon without seeing the connection between it and the teachers' common-language discussion.

Jean Lave (1988) also points out how we can denigrate everyday thought, even when it is clearly effective thought. All of us perform numerical manipulations of many types that serve us well, such as estimating amounts of different types of food to buy at the supermarket (where we balance many considerations, such as storage space in the refrigerator, budget limits, and the value of the particular goods on sale). School mathematics often does not apply well to these problems. Yet people will assert the general validity of school mathematics and not even see their own quantitative thought as mathematical thought. It is as if everyday thought is a grubby form of original sin that must be replaced by clean, hard ideas worked out in distant laboratories by people in white coats. Thus does common sense damn itself.

It is not clear that academic psychologists always have the high road to knowledge of how to engage students in learning. We do not mean that traditional psychological research is of no value. Indeed, we relied on it in arguing our case against telling students their failures are due to low effort. Must we, however, in the name of science, subject our intuitions—which reflect the wisdom of our culture—to a sort of intellectual boot camp? Common sense might not be the place to stop the study of education, but we lose it at our peril.[4]

Teachers should not, our study suggests, simply accept what researchers say. They should respect their own common sense. However,
if teachers appeal only to the authority of their *personal* experience, they
overlook the fact that their experience is not just theirs. They overlook
the extent to which common sense—which appears as the immediate
deliverance of experience, reality as observed—is a cultural construction.
Teachers are not just isolated individuals, but (along with academics,
journalists, and others) owners of and contributors to the big cultural
construction called common sense.

Common sense has obviously not solved all our problems, and it
never will. It needs to be reworked, in part through more detailed classroom inquiries, such as described in later chapters, in which teachers
and students construct and live better forms of education.

THE GAP BETWEEN KNOWLEDGE AND ACTION
IS NOT WHAT IT SEEMS

Our findings present a puzzle: If teachers really do know what our study
suggests they do, why is there so little teaching that would really foster
intrinsic involvement in learning (Goodlad, 1984; Newby, 1991)? The
answer, in retrospect, seems simple. We all *know* many things about
people, but we *use* only what is relevant to our purposes.

Teachers have many concerns in addition to student motivation. How
many schools are there where the principal prowls the halls hoping to
hear excited students debating ideas? There is little pressure on teachers to excite students about learning. Parents and principals are more
likely to emphasize silence and high test scores. When this happens,
teachers will tense up and become coercive (Deci, Spiegel, Ryan, Koestner, & Kauffman, 1982). They will not encourage cooperative learning
or student choice. They will avoid anything that could let students veer
from the things that will be tested.

Students also express the cultural pressure for high grades and test
scores. With grades and test scores in the forefront of their minds, students often resist anything other than the direct teaching of information
that will be "on the test" (Herndon, 1969; Jones, 1991; McNeil, 1986).
As one high school teacher put, "In my social studies department I think
that teachers have an adequate understanding of discovery learning,
cooperative learning, and the other methods . . . but they choose not to
use them because their students would not tolerate that style of instruction" (Kagan, 1993, p. 111).

What would happen if love of learning, instead of test scores or quiet classrooms, became a priority in schools? Presumably, if this really were a priority, teachers would not need to be told that reducing competition, for example, would enhance the love of learning. Researchers Maehr and Midgley (1991) thought it might be useful for a group of teachers to discuss the theories that suggested why competition might undermine motivation. But the teachers wanted to get on with reducing competition rather than talking about theories. Maehr and Midgley were surprised how quickly the teachers "caught on" to the drawbacks of competition. But perhaps the teachers already knew what undermines the love of learning. As in Pergande and Thorkildsen's collaborative project (see Chapter 2), Maehr and Midgley's project probably helped change teachers' priorities, making student motivation more important to them.

Perhaps an important function of all educational research, whether it is conducted by teachers or academics, is not so much to help us understand "what works," as if we already know and agree on what we are trying to achieve. Perhaps what useful research does is help us decide what we want to work toward, what we should be motivated by, what reasons we should have for learning, and what sort of lives we should make in school.

CAVEAT: GET SPECIFIC

We examined beliefs at a rather general level. We found, for example, that teachers and student teachers believe that letting students lead activities and have responsibilities will enhance the desire to learn. But there are many ways to interpret this suggestion. It might mean letting students help keep the classroom neat and tidy. It might mean furnishing a room with many books and telling students they can choose. Or it might mean presenting different theories of reading instruction to students and encouraging them to debate their merits, try the different approaches, and debate them again, and on and on in a continuous flow of action research.

General suggestions about teaching practices are only as good as the specific examples of them that can be created. Coming up with the general idea can be the easy part. It was one thing to propose a heavier-than-air flying machine. It took much additional time and much new knowledge to get one off the ground.

To get anywhere, one must be more specific than we have been in this chapter. This means dealing with the particular educational experiences of particular people. The remaining chapters in this book move this way.

NOTES

1. It will be apparent that the purpose of this study was not to assess how teachers think about motivation while teaching. They might or might not use their best knowledge when teaching, but that is a different question.

2. Dweck's (1975) study, which started this, was one of the articles most frequently cited in a sample of leading contemporary psychology journals (Walberg, 1990). (Citation frequency is widely taken as an indication of the influence of an article.) The degree of acceptance of the suggestion that students be told their failures reflect low effort is also indicated by the fact that it is repeated (as if it were well established) in the most widely cited of the contemporary articles on motivation in educational psychology journals (Weiner, 1979; see Walberg, 1990, for citation analysis). A casual perusal of educational psychology and developmental psychology texts will also quickly confirm that the canon incorporates the idea that it helps to tell a student who has given up in despair that a failure "means you should have tried harder" (Claxton, 1990, p. 140; see also, Stipek, 1988; other texts, e.g., Gage & Berliner, 1988, blur the important distinction—noted by teachers in our questionnaire study—between attribution of low versus high effort to students). Yet several university researchers told us, more or less politely, that no one believes that anymore. These researchers choose to ignore, or claim as invalid, textbooks and citation analyses. They deny the relevance of their own conventional research outputs.

3. This might account for the fact that the study by Miller, Brickman, and Bolen (1975) was almost ignored, even though it came out in the same year and the same journal as Dweck's study. Miller et al. did not wrap their work in the abstract language of attribution theory.

4. The argument that common sense should not be dismissed by psychologists, but kept in their bag of tricks, is apparently easily read as a suggestion that common sense is all you need. For example, Nicholls, Licit, and Pearl (1982) showed that it is common for psychologists to make real gaffes because, despite the advice of some eminent psychologists, they eschew commonsense readings of their own questionnaires. For example, they will develop a self-esteem questionnaire with items like, "I would describe myself as self-confident" and a masculinity questionnaire with items like "I am self-confident." When they find these two questionnaires are related to each other, they speculate about why masculinity and self-esteem are related. They completely overlook the fact that there are many virtually identical items on both questionnaires. In view of this, we (Nicholls et al., 1982) argued that one should not eschew a commonsense reading of research questionnaires. Yet there were a number of researchers who read our paper as an argument for using *only* common sense. One well-known user of personality questionnaires went so far as to call John on the phone to make inquiries about his ancestry and imply that he might know something about intelligence testing but that he obviously knew nothing about personality questionnaire research. We have no research on why this might be.

REFERENCES

Ames, C. (1990). Motivation: What teachers need to know. *Teachers College Record, 91,* 409–421.

Claxton, G. (1990). *Teaching to learn: A direction for education.* London: Cassell.

Deci, E. L., Spiegel, N., Ryan, R. M., Koestner, R., & Kauffman, M. (1982). The effects of performance standards on controlling teachers. *Journal of Educational Psychology, 71,* 169–182.

Dweck, C. S. (1975). The role of expectations and attributions in the alleviation of learned helplessness. *Journal of Personality and Social Psychology, 31,* 674–685.

Försterling, F. (1985). Attributional retraining: A review. *Psychological Bulletin, 98,* 495–512.

Friedrich, J. (1990). Learning to view psychology as a science: Self-persuasion through writing. *Teaching of Psychology, 17,* 23–27.

Gage, N. C., & Berliner, D. C. (1988). *Educational psychology* (4th ed.). Boston: Houghton Mifflin.

Geertz, C. (1983). *Local knowledge: Further essays in interpretive anthropology.* New York: Basic Books.

Goodlad, J. I. (1984). *A place called school: Prospects for the future.* New York: McGraw-Hill.

Herndon, J. (1969). *The way it's spozed to be.* New York: Bantam.

Jones, A. (1991). *"At school I've got a chance." Culture/privilege: Pacific Islands and Paheha girls at school.* Palmerston North, New Zealand: Dunmore Press.

Kagan, D. (1993). *Laura and Jim and what they taught me about the gap between educational theory and practice.* Albany: State University of New York Press.

Lave, J. (1988). *Cognition in practice: Mind, mathematics and culture in everyday life.* New York: Cambridge University Press.

Maehr, M. L., & Midgley, C. (1991). Enhancing student motivation: A schoolwide approach. *Educational Psychologist, 26,* 399–428.

McNeil, L. M. (1986). *Contradictions of control: School structure and school knowledge.* New York: Routledge and Kegan Paul.

Miller, R. L., Brickman, P., & Bolen, D. (1975). Attribution versus persuasion as a means for modifying behavior. *Journal of Personality and Social Psychology, 31,* 430–441.

Newby, T. (1991). Classroom motivation: Strategies of first-year teachers. *Journal of Educational Psychology, 83,* 195–200.

Nicholls, J. G. (1983). Conceptions of ability and achievement motivation: A theory and its implications for education. In S. G. Paris, G. M. Olson, & H. W. Stevenson (Eds.), *Learning and motivation in the classroom* (pp. 211–237). Hillsdale, NJ: Erlbaum.

Nicholls, J. G., Licit, B. G., & Pearl, R. A. (1982). Some dangers of using personality questionnaires to study personality. *Psychological Review*, *92*, 572–580.

Nolen, S. B., & Nicholls, J. G. (1994). A place to begin again in research on student motivation: Teachers' beliefs. *Teaching and Teacher Education*, *10*, 57–69.

Robinson, D. N. (1993). Is there a Jamaican tradition in psychology? *American Psychologist*, *48*, 638–643.

Schunk, D. H. (1982). Effects of effort attributional feedback on children's perceived self-efficacy and achievement. *Journal of Educational Psychology*, *74*, 548–556.

Stipek, D. J. (1988). *Motivation to learn: From theory to practice.* Englewood Cliffs, NJ: Prentice Hall.

Walberg, H. J. (1990). Educational psychology: Core journals, research fronts, and highly cited papers. *Current Contents*, *22*(13), 5–14.

Weiner, B. (1979). A theory of motivation for some classroom experiences. *Journal of Educational Psychology*, *71*, 3–25.

2 From Teachers as Experimental Researchers to Teaching as Moral Inquiry

Krisann Pergande, Milwaukee Public Schools
Theresa A. Thorkildsen, University of Illinois at Chicago

Krisann Pergande (in white) and collaborators

Perhaps the most significant learning occurs when we learn things we did not expect or intend to learn. On such occasions, we sometimes acquire not merely unexpected information, but new priorities. Here, what started as an experiment to compare the impact of different forms of feedback on student motivation was transformed. As initially conceived, the experiment encouraged teachers to treat students as objects to be studied rather than as people to care about. No one fully realized it during the project, but teachers abandoned this mission. They asked a new question about what sort of research is appropriate for teachers, and worked to form new purposes to guide their teaching. This led them to value students' experiences, their interests and potentials, and the content of conversations among them. This project and teaching both appear as a form of moral inquiry.

As an administrative intern in the Milwaukee Public Schools, Krisann Pergande was concerned about the low levels of achievement motivation among some of the students in her building.[1] During a course on motivation with Theresa Thorkildsen (Terri), she developed a plan to involve teachers in an experiment. Her plan was to encourage teachers to become more conscious of the motivation of their students. She also hoped to test how the research she was reading applied to the students of Milwaukee Public Schools, and show that teachers with local knowledge could more than hold their own with more remote academic researchers.

Studies of the effects of teacher feedback on student motivation attracted Krisann's attention (Butler, 1987; Dreikurs, Grunwald, & Pepper, 1971/1982; Miller, Brickman, & Bolen, 1975). According to this work, teachers should encourage students by labeling the things they do well and suggesting ways for them to improve (e.g., "You did a great job taking turns while you talk, now let's see if you can listen carefully while you wait"). Butler (1987) called this "task-involving feedback," and, earlier, Dreikurs et al. (1971/1982) had labeled it "encouragement." This type of feedback, they argued, would lead to greater intrinsic motivation. It would focus students' attention on their schoolwork rather than on their status relative to others. It would promote satisfaction with work and a desire to improve one's knowledge without fostering the desire for superiority over others. In other words, this sort of feedback would make learning an end in itself.

Teachers should not, according to this work, praise students for outstanding performance (e.g., "Michael is the best turn taker I know!"). What Dreikurs et al. (1971/1982) called "praise," and Butler (1987) called "ego-involving feedback," was said to foster a preoccupation with evaluations of the self rather than of one's work. It was said to promote selfishness, rivalry, and dominance, making learning a means to the end of proving one's superiority.

Too often, teachers are accused of not understanding research and not taking research findings seriously. Krisann understood these findings, but did not quite accept them. Milwaukee's low-income urban children, it seemed to her, have unusually low levels of self-esteem, which must be raised before the children can be intrinsically motivated to learn. That children would value learning as an end in itself when their lives are so

---

1. As is often the case when researchers work with practitioners, our collaboration does not follow traditional norms and requires explanation. Because Krisann was the designer and initiator of all the activities described, her perspective dominates and she is first author. Terri provided encouragement and a listening ear while the project was underway. She is also responsible for much of the writing. The names of everyone else involved in the project have been changed.

filled with violence and negative messages was hard to believe. Of course students can profit from the constructive suggestions provided by encouragement or task-involving feedback. But what Butler called ego-involving feedback and Dreikurs et al. called praise looked like what Krisann and her colleagues called "self-esteem feedback"—feedback intended to help their students feel better about themselves and experience pride in accomplishment.

Krisann presented her thoughts on this question to some of the Milwaukee teachers and administrators she knew. She asked for their help planning a study to check whether the research findings would hold with children from the poorer neighborhoods of Milwaukee. Ultimately, she and four other speech teachers and administrators who shared her reservations met to debate and organize a study to test their assumptions. The group was committed to conducting a traditional experimental study. Professors had told them that experimental methods were essential if the results were to be reliable and valid, and they had bought it. Nevertheless, members of the group complained that published research often fails to address their concerns.

"A lot of researchers come up with basic conclusions teachers already know," said Mrs. Aubry.

"Almost nothing is written by or with teachers."

"Teachers don't necessarily have to be told what to do," added Mrs. Brown.

"Actually, the Milwaukee Public School system is so large," said Mrs. Aubry. "There ought to be a lot more going on in our department that pertains to the population we have here! And, maybe it would make us feel a little bit less like we jump on national bandwagons whenever new things come out. Just because it's new, it shouldn't be that that's what we're going to do, and, therefore, it must be correct. We ought to pilot a few things and have people say, 'Did it work for you?'"

THE TEACHERS' STUDY

Traditionally, Milwaukee's speech classes had been structured according to a behaviorist philosophy. Students either repeated words after listening to a teacher or spoke in response to a photograph. If they did so correctly, they were rewarded. If they did not, they were corrected and asked to try again. Students' routine conversations, however, showed little improvement as a result of this approach to speech.

The teachers in the planning group wondered if this problem occurred because speech students were afraid to try their newly acquired skills in novel conversations. They thought that feedback intended to enhance students' self-esteem might help. Unwilling to give up their behavioristic orientation, they also thought that the feedback would be effective only if it served to reinforce skill-use (e.g., taking turns, listening, responding to others' ideas) while students engaged in actual conversations. The planning group, therefore, decided to work on improving the conversation skills of students with language and learning disabilities and to test the hypothesis that praise would be more effective than encouragement in effecting this improvement.

To make sure there were enough students, several other speech teachers were invited to help once the study was designed. The following, written in more or less the form of a traditional experiment, is the study.

Subjects

Twelve teachers and 60 children (grades 1–6) participated. The children were all enrolled in both special education and speech classes, and the study was conducted during speech classes. Seventeen children were in grades 1 and 2, 28 in grades 3 and 4, and 15 in grades 5 and 6. There were 47 males and 13 females. Thirty-eight children were African-American, 16 were European-American, 4 were Latin-American, and 2 were Asian-American. All came from lower-middle-class or poor families.

Procedures

Groups of three to five children were randomly assigned to receive either encouragement or praise. In the first session for each group, 15-minute conversations were held about a topic chosen by a student. Teachers, all trained in methods for listening to and recording children's speech, counted the number of times each student made statements and asked questions. (The teacher wrote, next to each student's initials, an S for each statement and a Q for each question.) Their goal was to record, as clearly as possible, the frequency with which each child spoke. They did not record the accuracy of children's diction or the content of their conversations.

For six additional class meetings, spread out over a couple weeks (speech classes did not meet every day), teachers gave planned feedback while the children held conversations. The teachers thought it would be easier to sustain a conversation if children selected the topics—a marked deviation from their tradition of deciding what students should say. They also thought conversations would flow more easily if students became more responsive to one another. While students conversed, therefore, teachers systematically gave encouragement or praise about their ability to take turns, listen to one another, and respond to the ideas of others.

Teachers used a clipboard, on which sample statements were written, to ensure that their feedback matched the intended treatment allocated for their group. Encouragement labeled something children had done well and encouraged them to improve, for example, "You listened carefully to what Cornelius said, now tell him what you thought of his idea." Praise ("self-esteem feedback") emphasized students' status relative to others, as in "Sharmon, you are one of the best conversationalists!" Teachers also told groups receiving praise that they were superior to other groups, for example, "You listen better than all my other classes."

The six treatment sessions were followed by a single post-test session wherein group members agreed on a topic and held 15-minute conversations while their teachers counted each child's statements and questions. Two weeks later, this post-test assessment was repeated.

Results

If the study had ended here, the results would have been generally disappointing to the group. Taking into account differences in children's pretest scores, the findings were in the direction predicted by researchers—not what the group expected. In all cases, children who received encouragement were more likely to make statements and ask questions than children who received praise intended to enhance their self-esteem. Most differences were not statistically significant. Students who received encouragement were, however, significantly more likely to ask questions during the delayed post-test than those who received praise ($F_{(1,53)} = 6.90$, $p < .05$). (See Table 2.1.) This suggests that encouragement is superior and that its effects are not ephemeral: They were clearer two weeks after the sessions than they were immediately after. Maybe Dreikurs et al. (1982) were right: Praise is not of much value—even for Milwaukee's low-income special education students, who so many teachers think need, above all else, a self-esteem boost.

WHAT DID WE REALLY LEARN?

If we had stayed with the original vision of a traditional experiment, our story would end here with some support for the hypotheses of Dreikurs and Butler. Yet this account would convey little of what happened or

TABLE 2.1. Frequency of Statements and Questions for Each Feedback Type

Feedback Type		Statements		Questions	
		Initial Post-test ($n = 60$)	Delayed Post-test ($n = 56$)	Initial Post-test ($n = 60$)	Delayed Post-test ($n = 56$)
Encouragement	M	40.81	43.72	3.27	4.44
	SD	21.71	18.04	3.32	4.38
Praise	M	33.12	29.90	2.50	1.94
	SD	20.47	19.72	2.90	2.46

M = mean, SD = standard deviation

what was learned. Krisann did not realize this, however, for several months.

Trouble began while Krisann was trying to compile and analyze the data. The members of the planning group suddenly showed no interest in helping her with the data that everyone had worked so hard to obtain. Had Krisann's behavior suggested that she would be responsible for this part of the project? Were the teachers assuming that this project now belonged to Krisann or did they still see it as a collaborative effort in which they had done their part? Krisann was hoping that the project would help teachers change their practice, yet she got the brush-off teachers sometimes reserve for university researchers. When she did finally analyze the results, only one teacher expressed more than a passing interest in them.

Another possibility occurred to Krisann. She began reading about ethnographic research and wondered if the teachers were uninterested in the results because they sensed the limitations of experimental research. Perhaps teachers were frustrated with the high degree of control necessary to isolate the effects of particular types of feedback and with the uncertainty of the meaning of the final outcome.

Wanting teachers to help her explore these speculations, Krisann organized a meeting to discuss the project after the school year ended and the pressures of teaching were gone. Seven participating teachers and two members of the original planning team participated in the audio-taped discussion.

Krisann had hoped that, by collaborating in studies, teachers would see problems with the way they teach. The fact that the teachers were not particularly interested in the findings made this agenda seem impossible. Rather than questioning her own agenda, Krisann hoped to clarify whether the teachers valued research and, in particular, if they were critical of such experimental studies. She did not ask teachers to elaborate on the concrete details of their experiences or on their reasons for avoiding the task of analyzing the data. Instead, she asked, "What are your thoughts on research in general? Have they stayed the same? Have they changed?"

Miss Cusumano said, "I can see why they use white rats and I can see why you rarely see research ever being done with entire classes. You know, they do child A, and they do child B, but they rarely do them together. You don't realize, when you collect data in groups, that you're dependent on getting four kids together at the same time. So, with these kinds of time lines, it drove me crazy."

"Research doesn't always have to be this pristine model that you think of the scientist measuring x amount of drops of something and putting it with something else. Research covers a vast area and so the point of all this would be to think about how we can do research in the schools that will still be considered good research and yet be useful to us—so we don't always have to depend on what someone from the outside says," said Krisann, introducing her own expanding vision of research.

The teachers continued with complex perspectives that were difficult for Krisann to interpret. They did not agree that experimental research was unhelpful and that ethnography was a better way to do research. Some teachers even seemed to prefer an experimental design.

"What do you think," Krisann asked, "may be some of the advantages as well as some of the disadvantages of doing group research projects like this—for us to do our own research rather than having outside researchers come in?"

"I had a heck of a time trying to do self-esteem [praise]," said Mrs. Gordon. "I really didn't feel I was doing it validly. I tried, but it didn't seem to fit with that group. And, I felt like it sounded a little idiotic to me. I guess I'm used to task-involved feedback. I had a hard time trying *not* to be task-involved.

"We discussed it with other teachers in the study, and there seemed to be a lot of differences in how we were actually doing the feedback. And that made me wonder if I was doing it right and made me wonder if we were going to get the same kind of results because we were interpreting the directions in different ways. I felt I needed a lot of structure for me to feel comfortable that I'm doing what everyone else was doing. I was a little frustrated in that regard."

These teachers were convinced that outside "experts" would do a better job of conducting valid research, but that teachers should be consulted about the questions to be posed. They expressed discomfort about the quality of the data and their cynicism was, perhaps, not without some basis. The real difficulties of running experiments in schools had come clear to Krisann as well. However, not everyone agreed:

"What do you think are the advantages and disadvantages of having teachers, educators, and building people involved in research?" Krisann asked, wanting to know if they thought they could still do research.

"I think Marie said it when she said we know best what to look for in conducting research. It would be a hit-and-miss approach to expect people from the outside to come up with it and pinpoint exactly what we need. It sort of reminds me of when we have speakers for in-service, and they aren't familiar with our district, or they don't take the time to become familiar. So, they spend the first hour on things that don't apply to us."

"I think whoever is doing it within the school system has to have some commitment, has to have some interest in it, you know, to be willing to go through the hassle," added Mrs. Gordon.

"*We* can get more valid results," said Mrs. Aubry.

"What might be your reasons for becoming involved in research in the future?" Krisann asked.

"Well, it kind of keeps me going, rather than, 'Oh, another year of doing the same old thing,'" said Mrs. Fitzgerald.

Mrs. Williams added, "Our self-esteem might be affected, you know. As a teacher-researcher you feel like you're really still on top of things. You're to help with what's going on in the field."

"I felt excited by it. By the discovery!" said Miss Cusumano. "I like the realistic attitude. We're constantly learning, and we're constantly looking for a better approach. It's a lot of work. I knew that going in, but it's worthwhile."

"*Very* worthwhile," the others chime in.

They agreed that, by participating in this study, they learned something about their teaching and felt excited by their discoveries. But what did they discover? They hadn't even seen the results! What a paradox. They showed so little interest in the findings, but felt satisfied with what they had learned.

LISTEN TO THE CHILDREN: THE *REAL* DISCOVERY

We learned more about this paradox from Mrs. Vanderbilt, who summarized the evolution of her concerns in a letter:

> I'm sitting at the monthly meeting for all school speech pathologists. Due dates, new policies, workshops, . . . wait, what's this? A research project? The not so distant memories of graduate school come flooding back to me. It's hard to believe I

was studying for comprehensive exams only one year ago. Maybe a research project is just what I need to get those creative juices flowing again. Nah, don't kid yourself. You can't handle the workload now. How are you going to squeeze *research* in with the already endless demands? But, what's this? I won't have to write lesson plans: The project is simple. I should do my duty to the profession and participate. Maybe . . . No, I have to learn how to say no. Okay, it's decided.

So, I'm filing out of the auditorium. A woman is standing before me, "You'll participate, right?" My mind is racing. "Well, I don't really have too many kids who fit the criteria. Oh, you say you can pair me up with someone who does? Okay, why not?" All right, so I'm a sucker for a good cause. Anyway, this may be a good chance to be working toward a common goal—the professional answer to study groups!

I'm sitting in this research orientation session. Now I'm getting nervous. Will I be able to pull this off without making any big, not to mention embarrassing, blunders? They need experienced clinicians here. After all, this is *research*. I'm just a pup, a duckling getting my feet wet. Deep breath. Okay, don't panic. Take a language sample, she says; I can do that. Direct a conversation; Okay, sounds simple enough.

I'm sitting here with my kids at the first session. They're looking at me as if to say, "Isn't this kind of silly, Mrs. Vanderbilt? When do we really work?" Stay calm. I need a new topic; think quick. They're looking at me to participate, but all I'm allowed to say is, "You are the best turn taker." I feel like a complete idiot.

Later in the project, the sessions start to go smoother. My kids are starting to get the hang of these conversations and accept the fact that I will not be interrupting them with corrections. I'm learning, too. Wow, I didn't know Jim wanted to be a policeman. I'm learning so much about my students as people and as conversationalists. Maybe it's working! Maybe we're all learning from this. And maybe, just maybe, an overwhelmed, first-year clinician *can* do research.

Mrs. Vanderbilt seems to have learned to see her students "as people, and as conversationalists." The experiment was designed to test an abstract theory about motivation and self-esteem. But she did not speak of this. She spoke of seeing students anew—coming to appreciate their hopes and ideals. Students gave up relying on her corrections and made the conversations theirs.

Looking back over the transcripts again and again, we finally saw similar themes in the discussion held at the summer meeting. Because Krisann was preoccupied with abstract questions about research methods and whether teachers could do research, she did not probe the teachers' personal discoveries. Still, the teachers spent a large amount of the meeting time describing these personal discoveries and most of them agreed that they gained greater respect for the purposes and priorities of their students.

Mrs. Schmidt said, "The study gave me an opportunity to see just how difficult it was for a lot of my students to carry on a conversation. How often they strayed from the topic or didn't take turns. I don't know, maybe in my usual sessions there just isn't that time to just talk because we're centering on the existing curriculum. I also found out more specific things, certain topics that they have more trouble with.

"That opened my eyes more as to the social difficulties they would have because conversation plays such an important role in socialization. And a lot of the students' behavior made more sense to me. So, I thought, 'If this is how they try to talk to so-called friends, I can see how they end up in a fight.'"

Mrs. Vanderbilt spoke even more explicitly than in her letter, "Well, I think I realized that I didn't really know my students like I thought I did. They started talking about things I could never have gotten them to talk about had I been in the discussion. They really opened up to each other. It's almost like they forgot that I was there, you know, talking about girls and all kinds of things that I would never have gotten them to talk about had I initiated it. Before, I'd been trying to get everything in the curriculum in, and it was rather like 'sit down, shut up, and let's have speech class.'"

It became clear to the teachers that students' reluctance to use their newly acquired speech skills could be attributed to a lack of freedom to converse about topics of interest and not to low self-esteem. This led the teachers to reexamine their assumptions about curriculum and to notice issues they had overlooked.

"A lot of these children," said Mrs. Gordon, "were used to speech and language type activities in which they get rewarded for the correct answer. They simply thought that every time I made a mark, they were supposed to get a point, you know? And, I kept explaining to them no, cause we weren't supposed to reward them for that sort of thing. They just wanted to get more points and it made me wonder about what kind of speech therapy I was doing. Maybe I was too structured for some of these kids?"

Mrs. Schmidt added, "Because the students involved in this project were LD [learning disabled] students, the LD teacher was interested in how things were going and how they were doing. I said to her, 'What good is it really to teach so and so 20 synonym pairs if they can't even sit down and carry on a conversation?' She thinks the whole curriculum per se is just pointed in the wrong direction for many students who have just experienced a lot of academic failure. I think it's made us both more committed to changing our strategies, forgetting the lists and lists of memorization. We now hope to help these kids learn how to survive in the real world because this is eventually what they are going to have to do."

"Well, I know my kids and I'm sure all your kids do too, they just love to talk," said Mrs. Fitzgerald. "And I always have had a conversation time where they can tell me what's gone on at their house. So this was kind of a natural progression of things, this project.

"Because it was natural, a lot of my kids really seemed to enjoy it. They took turns picking the topic. And if we didn't have somebody's topic one day, we put it on the list for the next time so they knew it was coming. My older LD kids really looked forward to doing it, having the talking time."

Like these three, many teachers said they became more committed to responding to children's diverse values and purposes. Yet not everyone was fully convinced. Mrs. Schmidt, for example, contradicted her earlier suggestions that the curriculum should be more relevant to real-world concerns when she said, "I have a real hard time working on this type of pragmatics because it doesn't seem like we're doing anything. Isn't that true? It seems like you're wasting your time. You're just talking and, you know, just goofing around and I think the kids feel that, too. You look at a worksheet as working.

"I know the LD teacher said she feels the same way and that the kids feel like it's all play. She'd do things, like she had them cook breakfast one time. They were responsible for bringing in all the food and learning the sequence. You don't want to make the eggs before the bacon. They thought it was a ball. The other teachers thought this was my way of rewarding them for something that they had done.

"Do the rest of you feel that way? If you're not sitting in a very structured situation with question and response, that you get the feeling that you're not accomplishing anything, that the students feel that way, and anyone walking past might feel that way, too?"

Is Mrs. Schmidt not ready to accept the legitimacy of establishing a learning community where students help define the purpose of learning? Is she reflecting the concerns of administrators who are usually preoccupied with discipline and test scores? During the meeting, Krisann was thinking about research methods and did not ask Mrs. Schmidt to clarify. Other teachers, however, gave advice. Their advice was about purposes—about the reasons for teaching and learning—not about how to make students comply with predetermined agendas.

"I always wanted my children to feel good about coming to speech class," said Mrs. Fitzgerald. "Whatever I could do to make them like the room, that was great. And we do play games, not a lot, but as a reward. Like *Language Land*, we're playing and it's a real learning type of game. And, they learn how to take turns and accept loss and you know, congratulate each other for a good answer or what it means to be a good loser. And, hopefully something like that will carry through as they grow older.

"So I know probably teachers go past my room and hear them shaking the dice and playing games. And I think, 'Well, too bad. The kids enjoy coming and they're smiling when they leave and if that makes them feel good, that's all I'm concerned about.'"

Mrs. Fitzgerald was ready to resist the pressure for silence and answers to multiple-choice test items. She felt satisfied when she built a productive community life for students and provided them with engaging learning experiences. Others sought a compromise.

"I had something like that with preschoolers, especially with the three- and four-year-olds," said Miss Cusumano. "We did a lot of play, play therapy. But, I find there's a way of structuring, too; to work on the pragmatics."

Mrs. Gordon said, "I think I wrote down here, when we were talking about how the kids didn't think they were doing anything, or accomplishing anything. I think a lot of times kids need to know in real specific ways, what it is that they're doing. You saying, 'Oh, you've improved,' doesn't mean anything to them. They want to see, 'Now I know nine when I only knew six,' and they can't comprehend it otherwise. So they can know when they're in speech it's fun and it's interesting, but it's accomplishing something, too."

In a responsive community, students must respect one another, listen to one another, and work to help everyone feel included. The children seemed to know how to do this once they were invited to direct their own conversations. The teachers, perhaps more than the children, had to learn to accept and respect students' initiative. Once they did, they were surprised by children's readiness to help one another.

"I'm thinking of this one boy I had, a fifth-grader," said Mrs. Fitzgerald. "He's just in the regular class, but he is a talker. But he rambles on and on and on. So this was real good for him, maintaining the topic.

He had a real hard time with that and the other boys would get on him. 'We're not talking about that. Go back. We're talking about Ninja Turtles today.'"

Miss Cusumano said, "I might find more opportunities to use peer pressure, you know, seeing as what I found out worked. The students can kind of get each other motivated to do things—on some occasions, even better than if you're a teacher giving it to them from the outside."

Asked to clarify she said, "Well, in one of my groups, a group of four boys, there was one boy in particular who just did not volunteer very much. But, in speech he never did. So, when they knew about the talking task, when they found out it was all conversation, that it was taking turns, the other boys used peer pressure to get him to respond, which I have never seen happen in speech therapy before. They would try various things every time they'd come in, like they had plotted how they were going to get this boy to talk."

These teachers' interest in the conversations of their students was an accidental benefit of allowing students to choose the topics to discuss— a valuable "side-effect" of planning an experiment. They became more committed to understanding and responding to the needs and interests of their students and found new, more personal ways to teach. In light of these new purposes, the official curriculum as well as the results of the study looked less useful.

TEACHING AS MORAL INQUIRY

Krisann and the teachers learned to approach teaching with new respect for the agendas of their students. They rediscovered the notion that "when the attitude of the one-caring bespeaks caring, the cared-for glows, grows stronger, and feels not so much that he has been given something as that something has been added to him. And this 'something' may be hard to specify" (Noddings, 1984, p. 20). They moved away from seeing students as objects to be manipulated and self-esteem as something to be induced. They began to see past preconceived agendas and assigned curricula to value the experiences of their students and to acknowledge and develop the students' reasons for learning.

In many respects, this study began with the vision of research David Bakan (1968) attributed to some psychologists, namely, that research consists of testing hypotheses:

> There is nothing intrinsically wrong with testing hypotheses. It is an important part of the total investigatory enterprise. . . . [But] psychologists are

often like children playing cowboys. When children play cowboys they emulate them in everything but their main work, which is taking care of cows. The main work of the scientist is thinking and making discoveries of what was not thought of beforehand. Psychologists often attempt to "play scientist" by avoiding the main work. (pp. 44-45)

The teachers learned, as Bakan might have wanted, that the most important work in both teaching and research is deciding what is important. Their inquiry was set up as an experiment, but the experiment became irrelevant. They began their inquiry with someone else's sense of what knowledge to seek and how to attain it, but established their own concerns as they went along. Nevertheless, it was only after the fact that Krisann and Terri saw the link between this project and what Norma Haan and her colleagues (1983) meant when they described social science as moral inquiry. As Rorty (1983) put it, social science, moral philosophy, and literature are all "attempts to find ways of describing our relationships to our fellows which help us figure out what to do" (p. 174). Perhaps the point would have been clearer if Rorty had said "figure out what to *want* to do."

We discovered that educational research is about our own motivation—about our sense of what is worthwhile to do and know. Had we recognized at the outset that we were engaged in moral inquiry, we might have conducted a better inquiry. We might have spoken more directly about purposes and reasons for teaching and learning.

Acknowledgment. We would like to extend our gratitude for the assistance of those administrators, teachers, and students who participated in the many phases of this project. Also we are grateful for the assistance of Fernando Delgadillo, Alison Seghers, and Algis Sodonis.

REFERENCES

Bakan, D. (1968). *On method*. San Francisco: Jossey-Bass.
Butler, R. (1987). Task-involving and ego-involving properties of evaluation: The effects of different feedback conditions on motivational perceptions, interest and performance. *Journal of Educational Psychology*, 79, 474-482.
Dreikurs, R., Grunwald, B. B., & Pepper, F. C. (1982). *Maintaining sanity in the classroom: Classroom management techniques* (2nd ed.). New York: Harper and Row. (Original work published 1971.)
Haan, N., Bellah, R. N., Rabinow, P., & Sullivan, W. M. (Eds.). (1983). *Social science as moral inquiry*. New York: Columbia University Press.

Miller, R. L., Brickman, P., & Bolen, D. (1975). Attribution versus persuasion as a means for modifying behavior. *Journal of Personality and Social Psychology, 31*, 430–441.

Noddings, N. (1984). *Caring: A feminist approach to ethics and moral education.* Berkeley: University of California Press.

Rorty, R. (1983). Mcthod and morality. In N. Haan, R. N. Bellah, P. Rabinow, & W. M. Sullivan (Eds.), *Social science as moral inquiry* (pp. 155–176). New York: Columbia University Press.

3 The Volcanic Mind

THE STORY OF SYLVIA ASHTON-WARNER

Marue E. Walizer, Princeton University

New Zealand, 1945

When research is seen as moral inquiry, it is not difficult to see the novel as a form of research. Walizer uses Sylvia Ashton-Warner's influential fiction and nonfiction to show that an individual teacher writing about her work can be a powerful researcher. In this role, the teacher shapes her own life and the lives of her students. Walizer explores the vision of motivation and learning Ashton-Warner creates as she struggles to name and tap the fears and hopes of her students and, at the same time, to shape and realize her dreams in a world where dreams are made to be destroyed.

As a young teacher, I yearned to understand how teachers whom I ad-
mired and wanted to emulate actually thought about their work. How
did they develop the ideas and activities that seemed to work so well?
How did they "think on their feet"? What for them did it mean "to teach?"
When I asked these questions, as well as when I listened to faculty room
exchanges, what I most often heard were stories of funny or trying episodes in the classroom, on the phone with parents, or with other teachers. Much later, as a veteran high school teacher and now as a university
teacher and administrator, my work has taken me to psychologists, philosophers, and educational researchers (Bruner, 1986; Dewey, 1929;
Jackson, 1986; Lightfoot, 1983; Schön, 1983) who have led me back to
that familiar form, the story. One of my favorite teacher storytellers is
Sylvia Ashton-Warner, in whose narratives teaching is simultaneously a
personal and a professional search, a process of reflecting the past and
reflecting *on* the past through story to provide a direction for future
action. In telling her stories, Ashton-Warner dramatizes the daily challenges of life in a classroom. One such drama concerns teaching students
from widely divergent racial and ethnic backgrounds. Another is the
nature of adult-child and, more particularly, teacher-student relationships
and how these develop and define an ethical teaching-learning situation.

SYLVIA ASHTON-WARNER

Born in New Zealand in 1908, Sylvia Ashton-Warner grew up in a large
family. Her father was sickly and her mother supported the family working as a schoolteacher, moving frequently from post to post, most of them
very poor schools. In her autobiography *I Passed This Way* (1979),
Ashton-Warner narrates her life in terms of schools, beginning with "the
first school I attended where Mumma took me with her at seven weeks
old and where I did my stretch in a pram in the porch" (p. 3). The sense
of prison inherent in "did my stretch" announces the ambivalent love-
hate relationship she had all her life with teaching. She wanted most to
be an artist and writer; she went to teacher training college only so that
she could live in Wellington and find work in an artist's studio. But when
she married a fellow student from the training college, she repeated her
childhood travels. She accompanied him, for over 30 years, to a series of
schools where he was headmaster and she was often the mistress of the
"infant room," a sort of preschool and kindergarten designed to prepare
children for formal schooling. Out of these experiences of childhood,
marriage, and work comes the drama, constructed in her books, of the

struggle to be artist, writer, lover, wife, mother, and teacher, a search for personal meaning, professional identity, and effective pedagogy.

TEACHER

Ashton-Warner published nine books, some novels, some educational descriptions, some autobiographical accounts, all forms of narrative, in the latter 25 years of her life, beginning with *Spinster* (1958) and concluding with *I Passed This Way* (1979), finished a few years before her death in 1984. Her lifelong encounter with what in her autobiography she calls "the bloody profesh" is portrayed in two works, *Spinster* (1958) and *Teacher* (1963). *Spinster*, the novel, is an imaginative evocation of how the idea for her teaching method evolves from a complex range of relationships and experiences over the course of a school year. The same images dominate both books and many passages in the two books are identical. *Teacher*, her personal account of her teaching method and philosophy, begins with the image that will come to represent the creative turmoil of her own mind, of her students' minds, and of her classroom.

> In the safety of the world behind my eyes, where the inspector shade cannot see, I picture the infant room as one widening crater, loud with the sound of erupting creativity. Every subject somehow in a creative vent. (1963, p. 14; 1958, p. 41)

This passage creates the sense of the narrator's emotional and psychological states, which permeate the action of both books. The "inspector" hints at her constant fear of official surveillance from school evaluators and "shade" foreshadows the importance that "ghosts" will play in her own thinking and in that of her students. The critical action takes place in "the world behind my eyes," the landscape of consciousness (Bruner, 1986) where her vision of the ideal infant room is born in the image of an erupting volcano, "loud," with creative activity.

This volcano image is the embryonic form of her theory of organic reading being worked out in her classroom and articulated through her narratives. The volcano's energy permeates both books, conveying a sense of the ferocity, the violence, the passion with which she regards teaching. The image compacts the narration about to unfold: It expresses her dream, the tension with the bureaucracy that inhibits her practice, and the theory she will develop, as well as the emotional intensity she experiences about it all.

Discovering and developing the imagery of children becomes the central methodology for teaching reading and writing in Ashton-Warner's infant room. The centrality of visual image in her theory is clearly evoked as a thesis statement: "Children have two visions. Of the two the inner vision is brighter" (1963, p. 32). The method is stated simply and directly:

> I use pictures . . . pictures of the inner vision and the captions are chosen by the children . . . it is the captions of the mind pictures that have the power and the light. For whereas the illustrations perceived by the outer eye cannot be other than interesting, the illustrations seen by the inner eye are organic, and it is the captioning of these that I call the "Key Vocabulary." (1963, p. 32)

This mind image generates another even more energetic image. The opening epigram creates the "landscape of consciousness" (Bruner, 1986) that the theory inhabits. She describes what she sees in her own mind as she describes the child's:

> I see the mind of a five-year-old as a volcano with two vents; destructiveness and creativeness. And I see that to the extent that we widen the creative channel, we atrophy the destructive one. (1963, p. 33)

The method is already narrative in form, a plot in metaphor beginning:

> I reach a hand into the mind of the child, bring out a handful of the stuff I find there, and use that as our first working material. (1963, p. 34)

The explanation of how to teach reading by this method is presented as a narrative and begins with dialogue, a favorite device of the author:

> "Mohi," I ask a new five, an undisciplined Maori, "What word do you want?"
> "Jet!"
> I smile and write it on a strong little card and give it to him. "What is it again?"
> "Jet!"
> "You can bring it back in the morning. What do you want, Gay?"
> "House," she whispers. So I write that, too, and give it into her eager hand.
> "What do you want, Seven?" Seven is a violent Maori.
> "Bomb! Bomb! I want bomb!"
> So Seven gets his word "bomb" and challenges anyone to take it from him. (1963, p. 36)

As a teacher, she intuitively uses the literary technique of an accomplished author to bridge the child's inner and outer vision. This is not at all surprising, considering that the teacher here, by her own account, preferred to see herself as artist and writer. What is noteworthy is her intuitive shift to using the artist's image and the novelist's technique of psycho-narration (Cohn, 1978) as a teaching device. The children are analogous to characters in a novel; she is the author plumbing their minds for the images that render what they know and think but cannot articulate. Teacher plays the role of narrator, finding the images that put the children's mental content into words, using the method to "read" her students' minds so that in turn she can teach them to read written language. The analogy between novelist and teacher is drawn in her comment at the end of the "theoretical" section; "I think the educational story is like the writing of a novel. You can't be sure of your beginning until you have checked it with your ending" (Ashton-Warner, 1963, p. 98).

But in the classroom she does not have the author's control over endings, though she sees the events as story and even envisions what might happen if her work is not successful. She frequently returns to episodes involving the violent young Maori, Seven, her "future murderer." Recounting the time when Seven's old stepmother appeared at the classroom door, she assumes the role of a character-narrator whose understanding is enlarged through the experiences related in the story.

"Come in," cry the children to a knock at the door, but as no one does come in we all go out. And here we find in the porch, humble with natural dignity, a barefooted, tattooed Maori woman.

"I see my little Seven?" she says.

"Is Seven your little boy?"

"I bring him up. Now he five. I bring him home to his real family for school eh. I see my little boy?"

The children willingly produce Seven, and here we have in the porch, within a ring of sympathetic brown and blue eyes, a reunion.

"Where did you bring him up?" I ask over the many heads.

"Way back on those hill. All by heeself. You remember your ol' Mummy?" she begs Seven.

I see.

Later, standing watching Seven grinding his chalk to dust on his blackboard as usual, I do see. "Whom do you want, Seven? Your old Mummy or your new Mummy?"

"My old Mummy."

"What do your brothers do?"

"They all hits me."

"Old Mummy" and "New Mummy" and "hit" and "brothers" are all one-look words added to his vocabulary, and now and again I see some shape breaking through the chalk-ravage. And I wish I could make a good story of it and say he is no longer violent. . . .

"Who's that crying!" I accuse, lifting my nose like an old war horse.

"Seven he breaking Gay's neck."

So the good story, I say to my junior, must stand by for a while. But I can say he is picking up his words now. Fast. (1963, pp. 37–38)

The simple narrative constructs the complex range of the teacher's knowing. We hear the language pattern of the Maori, the implicit story of Seven's upbringing back in the hills and the disruption of his relation with his "old Mummy," the obvious violence in his family, the problem of maintaining safety and order in the classroom with the angry five-year-old as a constant source of disruption, the teacher's own subtly violent response as she "accuses" a child of crying, the sense of community despite the differences in the ring of brown and blue eyes, and growing from it all the method of "organic teaching," her method of redirecting the violence to a creative end. Seven is "picking up his words. Fast." While aware of the unfinished quality of Seven's real-life story, she still gives her own story of him the "sense of an ending" (Kermode, 1967), a sense of event that has acquired meaning in a coherent context. This passage is used verbatim in *Spinster* as a key episode in the teacher's discovery of the concept of Key Vocabulary. In the novel's version the story continues differently after the "chalk-ravage" to make the point more cogently (1958, pp. 180–181).

The ending of *Teacher* provides a powerful image that transforms the volcanic energy that has rumbled throughout into a kind of sexual union and birth. Repeated intimations of sexual union and marriage close the section on life in a Maori school. Ashton-Warner calls teaching "an espousal," using the language of sexual union as the image for the ultimate fulfillment of her passionate commitment, and the image of the labor of childbirth to try to explain the integration at the heart of her thinking about her work.

When I teach people, I marry them. I found this out last year when I began the orchestra. To do what I wanted them to do they had need to be like me. More than that. They had to be part of me. As the season progressed the lesson began to teach itself to me. I found that for good performances we had to be one thing. One organ. And physically they had to be near each other and to me. We had to bundle in a heap around the piano. . . . There is quietly occurring in my infant room a grand espousal. . . . They don't know it but I do. They become part of me, like a lover. The approach, little different. The askance observation first, the acceptance next. Then the gradual or quick coming, until in complete procuration, there glows the harmony, the peace.

And what is this birth? From the orchestra it is music, and from the infant room it is work. A long, perpetuating, never-ending, transmuting birth, beginning its labour every morning and a rest between pains every evening. . . .

All the rules of love-making apply to these spiritual and intellectual fusions. . . .

I'm glad I know this at last that to teach I need first to espouse. And in coming upon this at last I find myself in a not undesirable company. I remember Andre Gide: "When I am alone I feel that my life is slowing down, stopping, and that I am on the verge of ceasing to exist. My heart beats only out of sympathy; I live only through others—by procuration, so to speak and by espousals; and I never feel myself living so intensely as when I escape from myself to become no matter who." (1963, pp. 209–212)

It is only after the fact that she understands the process of integration that has occurred. This imagery and the transformation it captures actually become the plot structure of *Spinster*.

This new understanding perpetuates rather than resolves the paradox of making the Little Ones part of her and at the same time becoming them. She teaches by inhabiting the minds of her students. Ashton-Warner's intuitive focus on imagery, on the captions in the children's minds, leads her to recognize the two dominant emotions pervading her students' mental landscapes: fear and sexuality.

These feelings, in turn, translate into her own writing. Because words "have intense meaning," the children cannot at first learn "bloodless words"; but her own intense and ambivalent feeling (both passionate and resentful) about teaching makes her characterize teaching as "the bloody profesh." The blood image carries multiple meanings; it gives life, it brings growth, its flow connotes both life and death; it conjures up fear, violence, and death. Here (and more clearly in *Spinster*) it is also the conduit that transforms the erupting volcano into a rhythmic, productive energy. The blood image, like the volcano and the sexual image, allows Ashton-Warner to organize and express various and often conflicting feelings and experiences about teaching and bring them to bear productively on her work.

The images of the volcano and of sexual union with all the associations of fire, heat, passionate feeling, consuming others and losing self, give a window on the way Ashton-Warner thinks of her work and organizes her teaching. *Teacher* closes with a section called "Remembering—A Story." The section begins with the identical passage that opens *Spinster*.

> What is it, what is it, Little One?
>
> I kneel to his level and tip his chin. Tears break from the big brown eyes and set off down his face.
>
> That's why somebodies they broked my castle for notheen. Somebodies.
>
> I sit on my low chair in the raftered prefab, take him on my knee and tuck the black Maori head beneath my chin.
>
> "There . . . there . . . look at my pretty boy. . . .
>
> But that's only a memory now. A year old." (1963, p. 216)

In the new building that has replaced "the heaving prefab," no sign of her work remains.

> It really is true that it has gone. It's just absolutely not there. Yet that rocky, raftered little barn with its melting frost and its vociferous company had housed my own castle; the Key Vocabulary that I had built as spontaneously as any of my Little Ones; block on block precariously, turret on turret, dangerously, with arch ways, stairways and cannon. . . .
>
> . . . All is sanity and silence and floor. I try to say something. . . . But my throat swells in that way when I see brown eyes when somebodies they break their castle for notheen: somebodies.
>
> . . . Sparkling five-year-old tears on an autumnal face. That why somebodies they break their castle for notheen; somebodies. (1963, p. 224)

Castles lovingly and carefully created are frequently destroyed in Ashton-Warner's narratives. One of the most wrenching stories, told in her autobiography, is about the destruction of the hand-drawn and hand-printed Maori readers, which she had spent years creating from the images drawn out of the minds of her five-year-olds. Having loaned the books to another teacher, she tells us that they were mistakenly tossed out and burned without having been looked at.

Teacher and *Spinster* both end in a moment of failure and depression, a return to the powerlessness of childhood. Yet the conclusion contains an underlying sense of faith that something of her work will last. What lasts is, of course, these narratives, which preserve the work of those moments, the events, the characters, and the feelings that made it all live. This provides "the sense of an ending," a defeat that in being *written* paradoxically suggests endurance, even triumph.

SPINSTER

The parallels between the nonfiction *Teacher* and the novel *Spinster* suggest how the narrative imagery of the personal account blooms into an artistically shaped plot that explores the psychology of a teacher and the evolution of a teaching discovery. Teaching is, in one of Ashton-Warner's favorite metaphors, "organic"; it develops and changes with the particulars of time, place, and people; like art, it is irreducible and individual. Yet we derive usable knowledge from such individual performance.

In *Spinster*, more than in *Teacher*, Ashton-Warner (1958) focuses clearly on "the world behind my eyes, where the inspector shade cannot see" (p. 41) and where the image of the fiery volcano, "one widening crater, loud with the sound of erupting creativity" (p. 41) becomes as much a description of her central character as it is of her dream of the classroom. The novel is a more deliberate transformation of her experience.

The first-person narrative details an extraordinary teacher's mind, how she thinks, what she feels, how she manages her work. The story dramatizes teaching as "questing," as "an inquiry into the world, self, and others from which personal understanding evolves" (Alberty, 1982, pp. 20–21). The novel form makes the author less vulnerable and allows her to "try out" roles while developing her themes of uncertainty, isolation, risk, and the inferior status of women that others have recognized in the lives of teachers (Grumet, 1983; Jackson, 1986; Lightfoot, 1983; Lortie, 1975).

The story is narrated by Anna Vorontosov, middle-aged, unmarried, a foreigner teaching in a remote New Zealand school. She has come to be infant mistress in a predominantly Maori school where she is the only woman on the staff. She is plagued by self-doubt about her abilities as teacher and as woman. Remorseful about not having married a man (Eugene) represented only in her memory, worried about her professional status because she seems unable to teach in conventional fashion, attracted to several of the men she works with but determined to keep her emotions in check, she is a woman with strong artistic and musical talents. She is often a pillar of strength to others, yet she is as much haunted by spirits as are her small Maori charges. Her great gift is an ability to transform these conflicts into an educational insight that becomes her "teaching scheme." Her own struggles with fear, sexual desire, and ghosts from the past direct her vision to these as keys to teaching the young Maoris unable to learn to read and write from European books.

Spinster begins with Anna Vorontosov's memory of her own voice, "What is it, what is it, Little One?", the passage from *Teacher* quoted earlier. But the scene quickly transforms to

> night when I am in my slim bed, away from the chaos and hilarity of my infant-room, it is I who am the Little One. . . . But memory only loosens the

tears. No longer does Eugene take me on his knee, tuck my black head beneath his chin and say, "There . . . there . . . look at my pretty girl." (1958, p. 3)

The frequent repetition in both books of similar words, phrases, even whole passages, points to common relationships and motives. "Little One" becomes anyone hurt and needing care: the children, herself, the young bachelor and new teacher Paul Vercoe who both annoys and sexually attracts her. Her own fear of professional failure and her repressed sexuality are constantly evoked by the ghosts of "the inspector," of the lost lover Eugene, by the young teacher Vercoe. These personal experiences prepare her mind and the reader's to recognize these emotions in her students.

Anna's resistance to teaching is overcome each morning only with a half-tumbler of brandy. This gets her going, literally across the yard and figuratively across the bridge between her personal world of art and fantasy and the public world of teaching in the school. The opening question "What is it . . . Little One?" is turned back on herself to become a search for understanding as well as identity. On one level, the narrative is about "getting through," serving not to solve problems (though it does recount the discovery and development of the Creative Teaching Scheme), but to describe how this teacher negotiates through a difficult time to an ending that makes sense of her experience. At the same time, it portrays a gifted teacher in the midst of her evolving work.

The narrative of *Spinster* is both a repetition and a rehearsal (Ricoeur, 1981). What it recounts repeats what has already happened and, in this case, what must be encountered again in some form. The narration of the first chapter weaves many layers of experience together: Anna's ambiguous, ambivalent, and often imaginary relations with men (Eugene, the Head, Paul, the chairman of the school board) in a world where she is the only woman, the tension between her teaching and her art. While her own mental landscape is permeated with talking flowers, riots of color, and music that reflect her personal internal struggle, the realities of the outside world, fighting and accusing in the classroom, lead her to reflect on the racial tension in the classroom. Those reflections in turn reveal the stances of the parents, the grandparents, and the community. The repeated use of long strings of dialogue from the children as well as Anna's responses frame both the cultural world of the school and her own personal sense of self, the major sources of the plot conflicts. They simultaneously convey her fragmented self-image, the multiple perspectives in which the children see and need her, and the many roles she plays with students age 4–16. Those same issues implicit in the dialogues of *Teacher* (1963) here are spelled out in elements of plot and character over the course of the novel. Conflict and paradox are developed in the images of her garden and her music. Music provides some mental peace and order, but these are constantly jeopardized by her sense of inadequacy.

Anna Vorontosov's sense of her fragmented personality, her own "mislaid" identity (1958, p. 22), is externalized in the 14 different versions of her alien name that the children try to get their Maori and white tongues around. Some of the names parody her sense of self: Anna Fail (her own name for herself), Popoff, Wrontossup (toss-up?), Wottot (what tot?), V'ront'sov (missing parts). When the Headmaster sends a young Maori girl who can say her name properly to help her, Anna reflects:

> That's what I like about Whareparita: she can say the name my father left me. And that's what I like about the Head: he sends someone to help me and he chooses someone who can say this name. . . . "Miss Vorontosov," complains brown Matawhero, "I'm sicka writing." A little Maori boy of six can say my name. I kneel to his level. (1958, p. 22)

Anna's recurring hope to do better is imaged in the renewal of spring that at the same time fills her with feelings of guilt:

> When the pre-fab where I teach comes into view, I run into something that does more than renew life in a garden. It is something you find on your shoulders with tight legs clasping your neck. I thought I had forgotten Guilt. I thought he was gone for good, and not merely into hiding for the winter. But oh, these precarious springs! Is there nothing that does not resume life?
>
> My song stops. So does my step. I lurk around the trunks like one of my five-year-old newcomers. If only I had done all that the inspectors had told me in the past—whenever they wanted me to, in the way they wanted me to and for the reason! If only I had been a good teacher, an obedient teacher, and submissive! If only I could have remained in the safety of numbers that I knew when I was young! But no, I've always been wrong.
>
> Yet it can't be too late. . . . Plainly the inspectors are all good men and all I need to do is to co-operate. What could be easier or more profitable? Slowly I will recover my lagging in the service. Then maybe this Old Man Guilt will release my throat and I'll be one with the others at last. How fortunate to have these chances! After all everything else comes up new in the spring: flowers and guilt and love. Why not my teaching? (1958, pp. 4–5)

In asking "Is there nothing that does not resume life?," the desired ending, renewal, is envisioned early in the novel. The questioning, however, reveals Anna's emotional stance toward teaching as prescribed by the inspectors; it captures the tone of pervading uncertainty and fear and establishes the tensions of fear and guilt as part of the renewal of life and of the drive to change. The paradox remains her desire to be one of the group yet to find her unique self—a real-life negotiation that parallels children's development in the classroom. These elements provide the plot deviations through which the transformation into a mature self that is paradoxically self-discovery will occur.

Anna initially characterizes herself as child and stranger, "like one of the five-year-old newcomers." Her language with its repeated exclamation points echoes the child's, desperately seeking approval from the father, trying to please and always failing. The inspectors, already characterized as ghosts, haunt her as father figures, demanding obedience. Infantilized by the authority figures around her, all of them men, she assumes all blame. She is not sufficiently "submissive." She must repent. She must do better, ". . . or try to . . ." (1958, p. 5).

Anna suffers constantly from uncertainty and ambiguity created by the demands of her varied worlds. These tensions in her own mind, to a degree and temporarily, are resolved in a passage that blends action, thought, and dialogue and reveals the interactive quality of thinking, discovering, adjusting, and being distracted.

> The thing about teaching is that while you are doing it no yesterday has a chance. If only I could get here! . . . After all I have only to cross the paddock through the trees and here I am saved. Why is the setting out so hard? . . .
>
> "Can I sit with Patchy again?" asks Matawhero.
>
> I look at him from my low chair in perplexity. This question has significance of some kind if only I could put my finger on it. . . . I have not yet wholly made the change from the world of the week-end to this one. . . .
>
> "Can I?"
>
> "Can you what?"
>
> Really, it's confusing, this overlapping of two worlds. Does it amount to a fall or a rise, this crossing through the trees?
>
> "Can I?"
>
> "I beg your pardon?" I brush my face more severely as though there were cobwebs collected upon it, obscuring my view. And to an extent it works because whereas before I felt there was some significance in this thought of Matawhero's, now I realize there is even more to it. If only I could see what's under my nose. I take a deep breath and concentrate. "What did you say, Matawhero?"
>
> "Aw, hell, I said it a hundred times. Can I sit with Patchy again?"
>
> Ah, I see it! Why doesn't he just get up and go and sit with Patchy under his own power?
>
> . . . Matawhero grasps both my knees and trains the full force of his brown eyes upon me. "Can I can I?"

So much asking! Who am I, the law or God?

"Why not, Little One?"

Patchy is pleased. His fair face lights up and every freckle sparkles. "You always want to tit wit me," he says.

Ah, I see something else! The brown and the white meet. Even though they can't mix. I brush my face again more effectively. Steadily those evenings of reading, Beethoven, Schubert, thinking, working, and remembering, move inland. Only in blood and by blood, claims my mind, can the races mix. Yet communication of any kind must be a step towards understanding of some kind. . . .

But I'm still not wholly myself. Not only the echoes of the music come back to me: the lethargy following the long and hard hours of work in Selah [where she writes and paints] this morning follows me. Plainly there are two worlds, and in which do I truly belong? Must I really drink myself through the trees over into this room of raw reality five times a week? No other job in the world could possibly dispossess one so completely as this job of teaching. You could stand in a laundry, for instance, still in possession of your mind. But this teaching utterly obliterates you. It cuts right into your being: essentially it takes over your spirit. It drags it out from where it would hide. (1958, pp. 7–9)

The passage captures the multiplicity of experiences as one teaches. First there is the layering of time, memories of past people and experience and of recent work, all coloring the present moment, supporting and conflicting with present concerns. The presence of Eugene, the inspectors, and Anna's need to drink her courage create a guilt that drives her to escape into creative work. The tension between two worlds is played out on several levels. In the "world behind her eyes" and in her love for art and music, she is alive and growing; in the "raw reality" of the classroom, she is fragmented and constantly unfulfilled. She shifts between the sadness produced by memories from the past and the forgetfulness induced by the demands of the present. She is insightful about the need to lose oneself in teaching and resentful of being constantly consumed by others. She lowers herself constantly to the physical level of the children, unsure whether this constitutes a rise or a fall.

This divided experience parallels divisions of moral and political power in her classroom and in the larger society. A child insists on asking her permission and approval just as she must seek the approval of the inspectors. Her preoccupation creates resentment in the child ("Aw, hell") who insists on her authority. She sees the child's vision of her as authority and seeks to diminish it. A brown child and a white one begin a friendship and she can momentarily see some purpose in her work. But her own sense of a divided self persists.

The verb *to see* indicates the multilayered nature of her narrative as well. She literally sees the concrete realities around her: the garden, the children, the prefab, and so forth. She also "sees" the stories and paradoxes that inhabit her mind about all these people and things: about Seven's Mummy and the brothers who hit him, about the rafters in the prefab that call up "the earliest memory of my mother," about Matawhero's proud grandfather who is chairman of the school board, about the flowers that bloom and will die, about her own house, "full to the top with emptiness . . . full of waiting past" (1958, pp. 11, 13, 15, 22, 27). Such paradoxes in the mind can only be articulated in narrative form. She "sees" in the sense of understanding when she reflects on Matawhero's request to sit next to Patchy. And she finally "sees" into the children's own minds when, at last, she draws from them the Key Vocabulary. Seeing on many levels is the central activity of the teacher's mind working as a painter with words.

A small aside here will demonstrate how the narrative clarifies the meaning of behavior. As a newly appointed principal of a nursery school, Philip W. Jackson (1986)

> noticed that when nursery school teachers spoke to individual children or listened to what they had to say they first descended to the child's height by bending at the knees until their faces were on a level with the child's own. At the same time, I was bemused to note, when I myself spoke or listened to a child I tended to bend at the waist rather than at the knees. As a result I hovered about the tyke like some huge crane, causing him or her to gaze skyward and, if out of doors on a bright day, to shade the eyes while doing so. (p. 76)

Jackson suggests that the teachers' bending at the knee to reach the child's height may have been an intuitive response to the physical discomfort caused when the child was required to look up at an adult. Ashton-Warner (1958) explains differently: "I kneel to her [a six-year-old girl] level; it's the least of courtesies" (p. 22). She honors the child, respecting the level already achieved. Ashton-Warner frequently describes Anna as kneeling to a child, also suggesting "becoming" like the child, empathically "entering into" the child's consciousness, respecting the child's own vision and intelligence, all of which Ashton-Warner sees as essential to teaching. Anna describes her own writing and drawing of the Maori readers as

> very simple. In the text and in the illustration I merely drop to their level. What they do, I convey. How they draw I draw, and how they speak I write. Their own mediums in meaning, line, colour and word. That's all there is to it. Simple. (1958, p. 186)

She uses the kneeling image to signal the shift from feelings of fear to beginning trust when the visiting inspector responds to the children's outrageous but hilarious comments.

> The shade in the rafters materializes into a man on the floor. Waking and sleeping, I have dreaded this . . . I am defeated. My contracting stomach proves that I am. I'm no brilliant innovator, no courageous champion of the young mind after all! I'm no more now, standing before him, than a manless woman. A woman with no background. No defenses, no backing or protection, whatever. Ah, return to the rafters, Phantom! Before these strangling legs of Guilt stifle my breath! Can I run away? Can a mother desert her children?
>
> Yet as he stands here . . . there's a kind of violent radiance in the prefab for anyone who can feel it.
>
> For one thing, an unerring barometer, the children approach him and for another, he doesn't appear to mind. As they stare up at his immaculate height I begin to suspect, not nightmare, but six feet or more of good will. . . . One-Pint gets in first. . . .
>
> "What you fulla come for?" he asks cheerfully.
>
> "I came to see Miss Vorontosov."
>
> "You her boy-friend?" inquires Matawhero delicately.
>
> "He got grey whisker," observes Seven.
>
> "Who's your name?" asks Tame.
>
> "How old are you?" asks Waiwini.
>
> "Do you gets drunk?" checks up Bleeding Heart.
>
> "He might be an Inspector," warns Mark. "My mother said you've got to look out for Inspectors."
>
> "I read to you, ay," Wiki nestles up to a leg-pillar.
>
> "Miss Vottot she haved her shoes off before play. She walked on her feets," reports some tell-tit most unfairly.
>
> "Yeah. Ay. An she got cootie in her hairs! I sawed her get it out I did. Mis Vontopopp."
>
> "Oooh! Miss Vottacock she got cooties in her hairs! Miss Vottacock!"
>
> Ah well. All is lost before I've started. If only he would kneel to our level! The rest of us are at a disadvantage down here. . . .
>
> But here he is pulling up a low chair too and sitting beside me. (1958, pp. 98–101)

Joining the teacher and the children near the floor, the inspector becomes an "enabler," and the immediate effect is the establishment of trust and Anna's assertion of self.

> He is remarkably quiet and unassuming for an Inspector, especially a senior. I can't make it out. Indeed, so open does he leave the field that I am constrained, uncontrollably, to talk to myself. And outrageously, that's what I do.

"I burnt my workbook," I hear . . .

"Oh?" He lifts his grey eyebrows. "Why?"

"Because I can't stand it any longer!"

"Why?"

"I'm not that kind of person!"

"No?"

"I can't do what I say I'm going to do! And that's what a workbook is. Saying what I'm going to do!"

"Oh?"

"I can't stand the planning of it. The clockwork detail. I can't bear the domination of it. I hate the interference of it between myself and the children, and I resent the compulsion. Sack me if you like! Sack me."

"We are not thinking of sacking you, Miss Vorontosov."

I am trembling and red in the neck. . . . What a way for a teacher to be caught! Sitting on a low chair holding a child like a woman! Why aren't I standing at the blackboard like other teachers with a pointer telling the children to be quiet and to listen to me? Why aren't I raising my voice above the room in authority? Ah, what a din in here! There are Waiwini and Wiki dancing on the tables to the piano music of Hori, come in to practice. What a characteristic failure I am! . . .

But for some reason Mr. Abercrombie has stopped right there and does not go railing on. Whatever is this miracle of a listening Inspector? . . .

"I keep a diary," I confide softly, passionlessly. "I am able to say what I have done. Waiwini, . . . bring me that big black book in the drawer with the picture of Ihaka on it."

I judge a man by the way he holds a book. At length he speaks. . . . "You must admit," he says reluctantly, "that this is the irreducible."

"I am irreducible."

"Apparently."

. . . "I bring them up on Maori books first," I explain. "They can't bridge the gap between the *pa* and the European school without it. They learn to read from books about themselves first . . . then they go on to the imported books. Waiwini, bring me that big white book with the picture of Ihaka on it. These are the notes of my reading scheme."

He spends some time looking into this while I wait. "How refreshing," he says quietly at last, "to find someone really thinking." (1958, pp. 101–103)

The inspector demonstrates the extraordinary power of "listening"; Anna insists that individual teachers, like good narratives, are irreducible, but nonetheless worth attending to and offers as evidence her books; he has the vision to understand these as her "thinking."

The structure of *Spinster* parallels both the development of Anna's teaching scheme and her personal quest for a productive life in terms that are "natural" and "organic." In the long and difficult "Spring," which lasts for 105 pages, the seeds of many stories and developments are planted. There are clues in Anna's drawings that will provide the basis for her later thought development, her dream of the ideal infant room appears, the lines of several interwoven and significant subplots are laid out including the stories of Seven, of Paul Vercoe, and the child Hirani with the turned-out feet. Spring closes with the first visit of the senior inspector (quoted above), whose sensitivity and interest in the teacher's work overturn her fears and fertilize the mental soil her idea and intuitions grow in.

"Summer" has 65 pages in which the planted images grow into generative metaphors. Anna's student helper Whareparita gives birth to twins, which shortly die, and this is followed by Paul Vercoe's suicide. Unable to deal with her own manlessness and childlessness, Anna represses all clues that point to Paul's fathering of the children. But her knowledge surfaces in "the creative vent." She begins to characterize the Maori reading books she writes and paints as her "children." She notices something in the children's writing that she cannot yet articulate until she recognizes the violence in her own books as she mirrors the children. In class, she observes "a strange excitement" come over one of the boys as he reads the word "kiss" in her latest Maori book. He rushes to show the word to another child and both light up and spell the word and tell other children about it.

> "Look," he says profoundly, "here's 'kiss.'"
> Why this sudden impetus in the reading, I wonder, putting up the words from the imported books on the blackboard for the day? What's this power in a word like "kiss?"
> But it is not until my mind is turned the other way and I am engaged in something else that the significance begins to unfold. Playing Tchaikovsky for dancing I see that this word is related to some feeling within them; some feeling that I have so far not touched. (1958, p. 161)

When the senior inspector drops in unexpectedly as he has begun to do, Anna mentions this and the conversation leads to insight.

> "It's got some relation," I say, "to a big feeling. I can't put my finger on it."
> "Do you mean it's a caption?"
> Caption! Caption! ... caption ...
> Caption. . . . The whole question is floodlit. The word is the caption of a very big inner picture. . . .
> It's the caption of a huge emotional picture . . . the caption of a mighty instinct: sex.
> But I'm so slow. You never saw anyone as slow as me when some-

thing is under my nose. It is a day or two further on before I see any more. I am bent double over the clay container in the storeroom working over the consistency of the clay when it comes to me that there must be other captions of a like nature. Other captions carrying their own pictures in the mind. . . . Fear, for instance, the only instinct I know that is bigger than sex. What is its caption, I wonder? (1958, pp. 161–162)

She ponders as she goes on working and talking with her helper. Her volcano of thought continues "as though some unstemmable pressure had been let loose within" (p. 162). She goes to the children.

"What are you afraid of, Tame?"
"The ghost," he says, his eyes changing.
"What are you frightened of, Patchy?"
"The alligator."
"What are you frightened of, Reremoana?"
"The ghost."
I try out "ghost" and "kiss" on the ones who can't learn to read. I print them on the low wall blackboard where they can touch them and Lo! The next morning here are these non-readers recognizing these words from one look the day before; children who have stalled on the imported books for months; on the words, "come and look, see the boats." Wiki and Blossom and One-Pint "an' them." Lo, here are these stallers reading overnight! (1958, pp. 162–163)

The discovery is followed by questions.

Ghost . . . kiss; captions of the instincts. There must be many more words like this, analogous to these two; captions of other instincts, desires, resentments, horrors and passions. What are they? How do you get hold of them? How do you plunge your hands into their heads and wrench them out? (1958, p. 163)

The school bell rings and "the delicate structure of thought rising block by block in precarious balance like the blocks I am always stepping over, is shattered . . . and my tower shivers and is lost" (1958, p. 163).

But summer is not over and she continues to study the children's writing. It takes six weeks of vacation and rest before the insight can be articulated to her satisfaction. As the school reopens, a conversation with the sympathetic and supportive inspector helps:

Somehow with all the talk during the morning he has afforded me in the infant room, the destruction of my thinking from the bell last year has been repaired and I see the tower, rising in all its preciousness and delicacy; the tower of thought that has been hovering above me, ungraspable for two seasons; this *key*. And it is no longer mysterious and nebulous. It is as simple as my Little Ones. The whole system of infant room vocabulary flashes before the inner eye as though floodlit. As I walk alongside the Senior, engaged in conversation on the surface of my mind about the regimentation in many schools, I am realizing what the captioning of the inner world is. It's the vocabulary I've been after. And . . . I christen it the Key Vocabulary. (1958, p. 170)

"Summer" closes with a feeling of "precarious peace," in which the idea, with the senior inspector serving as midwife, has time to develop. The sexual image rises again. The idea formed in her mind-womb required fertilization from another. The sexual attraction she feels toward the senior inspector alerts her to the sexual instinct in the children as Tame reacts to "kiss." "Summer" closes with hope and optimism; Anna thinks: "I am a Little One piling up a tall tower in the doorway. I am a teacher cleaving a track through the undergrowth of method. I am a bird. . . . Rebuilding" (1958, p. 171).

"Autumn" is the time for "fruiting" when Anna constructs a research program on the Key Vocabulary to test her theory. There is a growing coherence to her sense of self even as the activity level in her classroom and in the school heightens. The division between her sense of the personal and the professional begins to fade. "A cell in a brain doesn't speak for itself alone. And when you are one cell in a school brain you speak and work for the school" (1958, p. 175). Nonetheless,

> the reading is very much on my mind. All other concerns take second place. I must satisfy myself on this matter. Day by day I seek the most vital words for a child to begin with. So much hangs on the issue. The love of reading for a lifetime, for one. Day by day through the unrelenting testing these words sort themselves out. With alarming clarity they group themselves round the two main instincts. I'm thinking about it most of the time, either on the lower levels when attending to something else, or on the surface when I'm actively experimenting. I cannot see that there will be any break until I have found out all I want and need to know about the whole sad affair of infant reading. (1958, p. 176)

Anna then narrates her own thinking, revealing how retrospection brings a discovery, represented in an image of the transformation taking place:

> Plainly there are Key Vocabularies. They belong to children with some emotional impediment blocking the creative channel and twisting their

living. What with Rangi's "butcher-knife" and "gaol," Wiki's "daddy, fight, broom," Blossom's "blankets, mattress, cold" and Patu's "baby, dead, cried. . . ." What are these imported books imposed on the Maori infant room doing to the children in them? Even the white children, for all their respectability and painfully good manners and distressing concern with cleanliness, have their own exciting vocabularies. What a big new strange uncharted ocean I find myself floundering about in! For one thing the tone of the infant room is changing. It's making a transition from a series of explosions to something that feels like an artery rhythmically pumping blood. Something with the same force, but more natural, more comely. (1958, p. 178)

The transformation in the classroom parallels a shift in her personal life. The violent sexual imagery of the volcano, like the common outcome of sex, has become a life growing at a more natural, steady, rhythmic rate inside her mind and in her classroom. The image describes her theory of the two vents of the volcano (cf. p. 35): As the creative vent is widened, the violent vent subsides into something more normal.

Narrating another episode, Anna describes comparing the words she gets from the children with the words in the conventional readers, searching out more information about the children's backgrounds so she can ask the right questions, all the while feeling like a careful mother nurturing two delicate infants: "I've got two new things now, constantly needing my attention, in my Maori books and the Key Vocabulary. There are times when I feel like Whareparita with her twins, except that mine, so far survive" (1958, p. 177).

My twins.

My Maori books and my Key Vocabulary. Whareparita was never more thrilled than me. But there's no little white boxes at the bottom of a deep grave for me to weep upon. As the little babies should have done, the faces of my children are filling out and they're beginning to show real strength.

. . . I stride forward in the light. I take this Key Vocabulary in the morning output period when nervous energy is at its peak, . . .

I take it the minute they come in . . . I want to catch the first freshness. . . .

It's the easiest way I have ever begun reading. There's no driving to it. There's no teaching at all. . . .

Although Guilt never lets me forget his legs on my throat during the operation of the Key Vocabulary, I still know that by professional standards if not by emotional, I am free. (1958, pp. 181–183)

Her personal and professional transformation is evident in her sense of fruitfulness, expressed by the metaphor of birth, resolving temporarily the pain of her spinsterhood and endowing her work with radiance and the sanctity of life itself.

> There's so much to do and life looks short from my age. For here, quietly giving birth, right under my nose and without my having anticipated it, is my dream infant room.
>   . . . How many subjects in the creative vent now? Talking, dancing, the plastic arts, vocabulary, printing, writing, and now reading. . . .
>   Am I so irremediably sterile? Do I not breed too? True, my disappointed person clamours for its right to fulfillment but could a birth from the body possibly engender anything like this radiance of the mind. How can . . . any physical meeting with a male compare with an engagement like this? (p. 195)
>   . . . I believe that I have after all conceived in the spring just like any other of God's creatures, have carried developing life through the summer until now; here with the falling leaves and the reddened berries, are my dream infant room and my nearly completed books. . . . there is a relaxing of tension in the womb of my spirit, just as in any other animal. And in this at least I am like others. (1958, p. 207)

Now the senior inspector brings "visitors" to her classroom and the interest of these university professors energizes her even further. Anna speaks of

> the fine gift . . . . : the talking to my kind like other and normal people, forcing as it invariably does a progression in my thinking. . . . It's a tremendous step in my shadowy life. It's the biggest thing in it. This talking of all I feel through the medium of color and line and children's language to one who is listening. (1958, pp. 188–189)

Her theory proceeds to the next level. She now rushes to school each morning "with no trouble at all, and no brandy at all" (p. 190).

> At last I'm beginning to see what these surprising writings are that the bigger ones indulge in during the morning output period. They're captions too. Two-word captions: my shoes. Three-word captions: I want you. And story-length captions. I take up Matawhero's book. His letter formations are almost unintelligible, being a boy who does far more with his tongue than with his hands, and they are not made any clearer by frequent rubbings out and doubling. But I can read it. I can read him without writing at all if it comes to that. (1958, pp. 190–191)

By this stage Anna is unmistakably functioning like an anthropologist, reading the children like a text, creating her own text, and constructing with her students the meaning of what they do together. Ashton-Warner includes five or six examples of the children's writing, all life-revealing. Then Anna says,

> "Come and read, Little One . . ."
> . . . I give her her own manhandled page and to see her read this, her dug-in printing, her faulty spacing and childish layout, is to realize that legibility and expert setting run nowhere in the race with meaning. Indeed, it is to realize something else and it comes to me with the same relief from pressure with which the other realizations have been emerging: primer children can write their own books. They actually *are*.
> Moreover we'll read these books. Every day. . . . New and exciting books written every morning about the *pa*, with all the illustrations vivid in the infant-room mind already!
> Why am I so slow to see these things? This has been with me for a year and I have not seen it until now. (1958, p. 193)

"Autumn" closes, and Anna is back again "in the world behind my eyes" where there is an "intense . . . blue of a second blooming" (p. 209). "Winter" is contained in three brief pages. Anna's work goes on, visitors continue to come, her mind takes rest before the recurring spring "stings" everything to life once more. The form of the section embodies the sense of hibernation, of consolidation, before the process of renewal begins.

The final section brings "Spring Again," with a same-but-different Anna, tired only from the intensity of her work. A discussion with the senior inspector has him reading from the "scheme," which Anna has been writing all winter. The passage being read is about the volcano with two vents, one destructive, the other creative. The season begins in genuine happiness for Anna senses that she has finally earned genuine professional status, that she will be able to teach her method to other educators—until her official grading arrives and she finds "there has been no increase of grading whatever" (1958, p. 231). The humiliation brings her work to a halt, and a letter from the long-lost Eugene brings the plot to a desired conclusion. Anna leaves the school and New Zealand for another life and the final passage brings the story full circle to the beginning:

> "What is it, what is it, Little One?"
> A big man, ugly enough without the heavy horn-rimmed glasses, kneels to my level and tips my chin. Tears break away and set off down my face.
> That's why somebodies they tread my sore leg for notheen: somebodies.
> He sits on a low chair in his study, takes me on his knee and tucks my black head beneath his chin. . . .
> "There . . . there . . . look at my pretty girl." (1958, p. 242)

She is a little girl again on her father's knee, seeking comfort as she so often gave it to her little ones. The search for meaning implied in the question repeated throughout the narration, her identification with a child and the movement honoring the child's level both begin and end the movement of the novel. Coming full circle, the narrative closes yet goes on, focusing attention on "the complex relationships between self-growth and nurturing growth . . . essential to becoming a good teacher" (Kohl, 1984, p. 5).

There is no closure in real teaching. Each year begins anew; some of the past repeats itself and some things have changed. It is the teacher's task to make the transformation into something new yet coherent. The novel's structure is a metaphor for that process. It also narrates quite effectively the epistemology of practice characterized by Schön (1983) as "reflection-in-action."

NARRATIVE AS SEARCH AND RESEARCH

Spinster communicates several "methods" simultaneously in a discourse accessible to teachers—it is their own experience more fully imagined. The strong, semi-sad ending of the novel is an important element in reading the sense of teacher's thinking that Ashton-Warner is embodying in her story. The story can be read as a quest on several levels: the search for an "ideal" teaching method, the struggle to find a unified self, and the search for love and belonging. Each aspect of the search corresponds to a level of most teachers' experience: the professional level, the individual level, and the social level. Anna finds some satisfactory form of each of these, but not perfectly. This is fiction but not a fairy tale.

The ending seems dictated in part by Ashton-Warner's own failure to make any impression on the New Zealand educational authorities, but it captures the experience of the many teachers whose work goes unnoticed, who struggle to reach the child's level and to use the power of the mind's volcanoes. At the same time, paradoxically, the novel's great international success belies the failure and again demonstrates the importance of narrative to preserving the important work the teacher has done.

These stories of work lost or destroyed, "broken for notheen," seem a powerful metaphor for another aspect of the experience of teaching. Teachers rarely see concrete or continuing results of their work. They must continue to teach in spite of constant uncertainty about the value or the results of their efforts (Jackson, 1986, pp. 53ff.). Ashton-Warner copes with this paradox and uncertainty as teacher-writer. By closing *Teacher* with the last line of the stanza of the *Rubaiyat*, she records her faith in the power of the narrative text:

> The Moving Finger writes: and, having writ
> Moves on: nor all your Piety nor Wit
> Shall lure it back to cancel half a Line,
> Nor all your Tears wash out a Word of it.

The novel provides a richer, clearer account of the teaching method set out in *Teacher* by reinventing the process of its development and bringing the reader into that experience. It is "explanatory" as well as "descriptive." The images of the volcano, of sex and birth, used as metaphors in *Teacher*, are woven into the thought and language of *Spinster* as part of Anna's developing investigation on how learning occurs and her effort to create in her classroom a viable life for the children and for herself. This makes education a process of conception, birth, and growth —and death is also an acknowledged part of the story.

This belief about teaching and learning goes beyond the commonly used sense of "organic" as an educational metaphor. Although Ashton-Warner (1979) was deeply influenced by Rousseau and *Emile* was the first "educational" book that she found compatible with her own experience (pp. 194–195), the theory implicit in *Spinster* goes beyond the concept of "natural" development. The novel envisions teaching as a form of dynamic energy, some of it sexually driven, that creates and consumes. The teacher here is not merely the gardener nurturing young growth, though surely that is essential; the teacher here is a creator, an intellectual earth mother whose own ideas require fertilization through exchange with others in a kind of intellectual intercourse through which she is also reborn.

Believing that children come to school with genuine knowledge and powerful motives, Ashton-Warner's teacher must uncover that knowledge and use those urges to bridge the child's world with the larger world. *Spinster* describes how closely the process of doing that parallels a teacher's own growth and development—at any age. This parallel process of personal development and professional growth is captured artistically in the narrative structure, which provides simultaneous, multiple levels of meaning through its use of imaginative rather than literal language. The storytelling is a search for meaning that leads to a discovery of the teachers' own construction rather than to a preexisting answer.

The relevance of narrative-making to the development of a strong sense of self is discussed by Hayden White (1981), a philosopher of history who suggests that the growth of narrative is parallel to the growth of the concept of person and of legal rights. Madeline Grumet (1983) has also argued that a strong narrative voice indicates a similarly strong sense of creativity in making a meaningful life. Grumet claims:

> The maternal ethos of altruism, self-abnegation, and repetitive labor has created a class of persons with little narrative capacity, for to tell a story is to impose form on experience. Deprived of the opportunity to design the structures of their own lives, many women, mothers, and teachers, live through other people's stories. Having relinquished their own beginnings, middles, and ends, they are attracted to soap operas whose narratives are also frequently interrupted, repetitive, and endless. (p. 34)

That insight is supported in Sylvia Ashton-Warner's (1979) autobiography when she describes her own nervous breakdown and subsequent recovery through carving out time, with her husband's help, to devote to writing and drawing (pp. 275ff.).

Teaching in this perspective is ultimately a deeply personal and intimate activity as well as a public and professional one. In the novel, hard work is requisite in and out of the classroom. Winter, the fallow time, takes only three pages, and spring always returns to insist on beginning again. In Ashton-Warner's vision of what it means to teach, the teacher's own sense of who she is goes on the line every day.

Bringing coherence to the self is part of the narrative enterprise. These stories make that clear. Good teaching seems, at least in part, the expression of a strong individual self, strong enough to lose itself in others without being really lost, strong enough to grow through the challenge of genuine interaction. Ashton-Warner's novel develops that vision of teaching more fully because, as a "fiction," it makes her as teacher and writer less vulnerable.

It seems clear to me that developing good programs of teacher education requires listening to teachers' stories and educating teachers to do the same with their students. Developing one's own narrative voice should be as much a part of the training and development of teachers as the history of education, theories of human development, and the psychology of learning. By learning to tell better stories, we articulate what we know, evaluate our work, enlarge the body of knowledge about our work, and become better teachers. The bonus is that process changes not only life in the classroom but also one's own life.

REFERENCES

Alberty, B. (1982). Children's art: Where art and education meet. *Artworkers-News, 11*, 20-21.

Ashton-Warner, S. (1958). *Spinster*. New York: Touchstone/Simon and Schuster.

Ashton-Warner, S. (1963). *Teacher*. New York: Touchstone/Simon and Schuster.

Ashton-Warner, S. (1979). *I passed this way*. New York: Alfred A. Knopf.

Bruner, J. (1986). *Actual minds, possible worlds*. Cambridge: Harvard University Press.

Cohn, D. (1978). *Transparent minds: Narrative modes for presenting consciousness in fiction*. Princeton: Princeton University Press.

Dewey, J. (1929). *Sources of a science of education*. New York: Liveright.

Grumet, M. R. (1983). The line is drawn. *Educational Leadership, 40*, 29-38.

Jackson, P. W. (1986). *The practice of teaching*. New York: Teachers College Press.

Kermode, F. (1967). *The sense of an ending: Studies in the theory of fiction*. New York: Oxford University Press.

Kohl, H. (1984). *Growing minds: On becoming a teacher*. New York: Harper and Row.

Lightfoot, S. L. (1983). The lives of teachers. In L. Shulman and G. Sykes (Eds.), *Handbook of teaching and policy* (pp. 241-260). New York: Longman.

Lortie, D. C. (1975). *Schoolteacher: A sociological study*. Chicago: University of Chicago Press.

Ricoeur, P. (1981). Narrative time. In W. J. T. Mitchell (Ed.), *On narrative* (pp. 165-186). Chicago: University of Chicago Press.

Schön, D.A. (1983). *The reflective practitioner: How professionals think in action*. New York: Basic Books.

White, H. (1981). The value of narrativity in the representation of reality. In W. J. T. Mitchell (Ed.), *On narrative* (pp. 1-23). Chicago: University of Chicago Press.

4 "Hey, man, why do we gotta take this . . . ?"

LEARNING TO LISTEN TO STUDENTS
Lee C. Colsant, Jr., University of Illinois at Chicago

Students and Lee Colsant, Jr.

Lee Colsant's transformation as a teacher is provoked by daily experiences with his African-American students and by two pieces of research. One piece of research focused on working-class English students and the other on white Americans whose experiences were worlds apart from those of Lee's students. This does not prevent the research from helping Lee to see his particular students anew, and to question the purposes that guide his teaching. He comes to respect and appreciate the students he had despised and who had despised him and his curriculum. Can education be reformed without individual teachers becoming more critical of their own motives and confronting students in more honest ways?

September's fresh winds announce autumn. Leaves begin a hint of their deep coloration. Stores still advertise their frantic "Back to School Sales." For students these brisk mornings carry the happy voices of friends as they board buses, bicycle through the streets, walk the sidewalks that lead to school. School hallways fill with bustle, happy greetings, and heartfelt exchanges. Amid the hugs, hand slaps, and the screaming "Good morning Ms. . . . ," "Good morning Mr. . . . ," the corridor bells announce their own contrapuntal themes. "Learning" pushes summer aside as formal school knowledge cuts into its sparkle.

"All right, students, please settle down; summer is over."

"I'd like to begin by reviewing . . ."

"Remember that in any right triangle, the square of the length of the hypotenuse equals the sum. . . ."

"Furthermore, the dates of the First World War are very important."

"And since travel is much more common, Je dois vous dire que ce sont les. . . ." Isolated fragments of knowledge multiply.

There has been nationwide talk about reform. This small word creates monuments of debate. Political flares go up every election year. Scholarly journals hurl points and counterpoints. There is the annual trumpeting of "Golden Apple Award" winners by local newspapers designed to inspire teachers. Yet, students year after year routinely push through the same revolving doors and face the same school knowledge. Reform? Like the 747s that fly over my school, it never lands here.

I have taught French for 17 years. The language and culture capture me. They also speak to students throughout the world. From folklore of the Middle Ages to the lore of Françoise Sagan; from Louis XIV to Charles de Gaulle; from Racine and Corneille to Anouilh and Beckett; from Voltaire and Rousseau to Sartre and Camus; from Manet and Monet to Chagall and Braque—a rich culture, a rich curriculum.

For me here there is satisfaction in contributing to a student's life. To witness a student thinking in French for the first time renews me as it does them. I feel a singular excitement when my advanced students discover the meaning in St. Exupéry's metaphor of the rose, its theme of human responsibility. These students become my "chosen few." They are the ones who struggle beyond dry grammar to share the imaginative world of literature—the ones I touch and who touch me. There is not the "you" out there, but only "we." This to me is teaching. Meaning is shared and savored. The bravado of school's extracurricular activities pale.

Like my fellow teachers, I also satisfy administrative needs: patrol the halls, attend meetings on discipline, on attendance procedures, on curriculum, student dress codes, student councils, parent conferences, teacher evaluation and on. In the midst of all that, I teach. I have had my "successes" in teaching. My students have won medals in Chicago's academic Olympics. They have won scholarships and have spent summers in France. I have added superior ratings to my portfolio year after year. They trace back to my first years of teaching in Quebec when I was alive with teaching. I felt close to my students then. Now I live with distance. The rendezvous I had with teaching has changed. I barely noticed my cherished discipline being smothered.

MY CURRICULUM QUESTIONED

So here I am, an Italian-American teacher of French culture, teaching African-American high school students from a lower-middle-class Chicago community. My classroom is flavored with posters of Paris, the Eiffel Tower, the cathedral of Notre Dame, the Louvre, Versailles, the Rhone Valley, the Alps—all to transport the newcomer into the heart of France.

I begin this year no differently than others. I introduce myself. The students introduce themselves with their own teenage chattering. Then, I distribute books. They can't wait to get their hands on them and scan pictures. They love new books, but are accustomed to used ones. Next comes my three-paged, single-spaced, typewritten, and, I like to think, well-honed syllabus with its course content, academic expectations, rules of conduct, and corresponding sanctions. Then I get to work.

I start with the newness of typical French names. Some students adopt French names—Natalie, Jean Pierre, Nicole, Françoise. They enjoy the mystique. Next, the typical French salutations—"Bonjour," "salut," "comment ça va?"—with the short cultural interlude on the custom of kissing on both cheeks. Some try it. The double embrace provokes laughter. Ripples of excitement spread. There are also the impatient, testing questions: "How do you say 'hot sex' in French?" Perhaps this draws them to the language. But not all students share this excitement. Some are in class only to make up credits for graduation. The school's program office put them here.

When someone calls, "Hey, man, why do we gotta take this shit for?" I know I've got something different. Some students know how to take advantage of the moment. I continue teaching, pretending I don't hear, hoping they do not extinguish the sparks of excitement in others.

This year my hopes are dashed. During the next few weeks, my well-honed syllabus fails to achieve its effect. I encounter resistance. A tug of war ensues. The few, who are willing to handle the rigors of systematic grammar drills and memorization of vocabulary, take a back seat to a growing, vocal minority. The novelty of French wears off. Yet, committed to my well-honed syllabus, I faithfully discharge my teaching routine.

As the weeks go by, the tension becomes more evident—always these petty, irritating disturbances. I find it distasteful to teach this first-period class. I resent their boldness, indifference, and constant interruptions. When I need collaboration for oral group recitations, I get calculated interference, challenges that can't be named. There are these background conversations, quick, turnaround chats, flying messages, late arrivals, and spurious disturbances. I resort to written exercises and supervise their seat work with authoritarian eyes. Silence substitutes for collaboration. I see the resistance of the angry ones entrench while the faces of the excited fade. I feel challenged from all sides. So I use the system's way to cure the problem. I regularly dismiss the ringleaders to the discipline office. I dismiss the student if I see any possibility of a conflict. Yet, sometimes I don't even face confrontations out of fear of some unpredictable retaliation. They couldn't care less about learning French. They have their own calculated agenda. But mine is legitimate, so I cling to it.

I had decided to do some graduate course work in the evening. I enrolled in a course where we read Paul Willis's (1977) *Learning to Labor* and Linda McNeil's (1986) *Contradictions of Control*. I find Willis insightful and captivating. He speaks of resistance by a group of English teenagers who call themselves the "lads," troublemakers who make every teacher's life a misery. I can relate to that. I am experiencing misery with my first-period class. McNeil describes how high school teachers develop teaching strategies to prevent classroom "chaos" at the expense of inquiry and shared meaning; how they reduce learning to memorization of disconnected facts; how fragmentation of the curriculum produces passive but alienated learners. I do not relate to that. I find McNeil's rendition of her observed teaching irritating and pompous. I continue, unaffected by these books. To accept McNeil's claim that teachers maintain control of students with grades or by reducing topics to "fragments or disjointed pieces of information" (p. 167) is far-fetched. To hear her describe any teacher's chosen curriculum as a tool of control is insulting. My French curriculum has deep meaning—meaning I want to share. To agree with her that teachers use, to coin her term, *defensive teaching* strategies (1986, p. 158) to turn the student into a "consumer rather than active learner" (p. 192) is to me ivory-tower talk. Yet I admit there are moments when I place students in a consumer-like position. But is my French teaching only that? Her implication that teachers perform—that I perform—incognito as some sort of long arm of the school administration seems contrived and ludicrous. My curriculum is legitimate. My methods are sound.

But September's excitement is fading faster than autumn. It is clearer with each passing day that I have some students who are not willing to accept my curriculum and are not at all threatened by me. They become real like the resistant lads of Willis, lifelike, no longer just characters of bookish reality. For Willis's lads, school is drudgery, offering no adventure. To be a student is to surrender to school texts, tests; to be passive—and they want none of that. These lads hold their own values, opposed to the school's. The picture slowly clears. I soon find my students have that texture of Willis's lads. It's this constant opposition I am being pushed to feel. I begin to see the conspiratorial nods of Willis's lads in mine—my countercultural intelligentsia of the street. Their unwritten code is simple: Undermine the control systems that I use and to which I cling. I am the imperialist they relish resisting.

The lads have no trouble winning the respect of the class. They are the ones in control. Charles, with his tee shirt, unbuttoned jean jacket, blue jeans, gym shoes, is their leader. Gold chains hang around his neck—symbols of his real status and power. His gumby hairstyle, slanted and parted, shouts his affiliation to African-American teenage culture. With deep, black, piercing eyes and assured stride, he commands attention as he enters the classroom. It's his stage. He enjoys the moment. The room itself seems to await him while I burn with resentment.

Here, in my first-period class, they begin their day. Charles joins Dion, Erick, Shaid, Tralon, Naim, William, and Aaron in the back corner—their turf to discuss the latest activity. All have that hard maturity of the street. Waiting for the right moment, they slip messages to Charles. He might respond openly or clandestinely. I often say nothing, avoiding confrontation for fear of their open ridicule or embarrassment. He leads their adventures. Somehow I feel Charles knows he will face a Waterloo with me. That does not bother him; in fact, it lends credibility to his masculine leadership. Charles has summed me up. His years in school dealing with teachers, I'm sure, contribute to that skill. And I, entrenched in standard school procedures, am unwilling to admit his power or acknowledge his individuality. He senses my estrangement and entrenchment. He understands the curricular game being jammed down his throat. That is what brings the lads together in defiance. The battle for ownership of the classroom takes on anything but subtlety. With me Charles makes it flare. Day after day he sends or receives messages. Some reach my ears intentionally; some inadvertently. Often I am left to wonder. Today is one of those days.

"Students, would you open your books to the section on the use of the partitive article, page 23," my teaching begins.

"Who the fuck cares about the partitive article?" emerges from their turf.

If I ask who said it, they would only point to each other in laughter. I dismiss it as I have in the past. But I see Dion and Charles in conversation. Leaning to Dion, I overhear Charles whisper from the corner of his mouth "This is one nigger he's gonna love to hate." I cannot be sure if I'm the "he" who will love to hate, but he is already close to the truth—I don't love him. Who else could he mean? Did I come in at the end of a conversation not directed at me? I can't be sure. It's just what he would throw at me, but I'd rather not hear it. I am more interested in ending the class period than in understanding him or them. I hate this first period. With each day, my stomach tightens and gnaws.

The lads haunt me as October wears on. When one finds his own ingenious way to be absent, I'm relieved. I could not care less whether I might be the cause of the absenteeism. To admit a pathology in my own teaching is not in the cards. My finger points to their lack of interest in any school curriculum.

My own evening course work was going as usual. Willis and McNeil are still discussed, but I give them textbook homage. To hear McNeil's (1986) point that the school's "control of knowledge has as its objective, control of the students" (p. 167) still annoys me. But her critique of teachers' teaching isolated skills and fragmentary facts begins to strike a chord. I think of grammar drills, substitution drills, repetition drills, memorization of vocabulary, exercise worksheets—all the "right stuff." I'm caught in a paradox. To learn a foreign language, drills (I tell myself) are needed. Yet they can be a clever tool of control. Am I using my methodology of teaching at cross-purposes against the lads? Am I using my lads? Do they see school as McNeil sees it—isolated, dull, bits of information, devoid of meaning? Slowly I admit a flaw in my teaching. Yes, I reason, as a schoolteacher, I am a giver of directives, the stopper of students in the halls, the admonisher of vulgar and ill-mannered louts—the moralist prescribing what society deems necessary. I am earnest in my objective to benefit the student, yet my efforts harmonize too well with administrative needs for classroom order. The lads see us benefiting. The other students see their reward down the road. They accept school routine and conformity with little resistance in hope of a brighter day. Must it all be a means to an end?

At 7:30 each morning, 1,500 students file through the school's main entrance. A teacher greets them with "all right, get 'em out [ID's], put 'em on, let's keep movin'." Students are daily herded into classrooms. In walks down the halls, room after room displays students silently doing seat work. Yet I resist McNeil's claim that teachers maintain discipline by the ways they present course content. It's arrogant of her to sit in judgment of teachers. Her talk of a democratic classroom is the fancy talk of academics. "Why doesn't she get into the trenches with us? See what it's really like."

Yet, somehow I feel that my teaching may not be truly engaging. The ploys designed to keep most students in their seats are not working with the lads—are not worth much for anyone. I concede my use of manipulative strategies. For what other reason would I instantly dismiss the lads to the discipline office? I come face to face with the illusion that I am contributing to the well-being of my students. The thought that I am an agent of the administration and that the student's welfare is secondary begins to take root. Is my act of teaching a mirage?

The first marking period winds down—finally. It is late November. Thursday afternoon begins parent conference day. Grades are given. It's my moment to let the lads know where they stand. I shoot one of my big guns of curriculum control. I give Charles and most of the lads failing grades. The parents hustle in, sign the tally sheets, stop for short, polite conversations and leave with their son's or daughter's grade. Just one of the lads' parents shows. I expect none. They must have seen Fs for years. The bland, hurried conferences drag. It is 7:30; time to go home. I close with the lads and McNeil on my mind. As I shut the door behind me, I wonder if I too have earned an F. I do not want to continue this way.

My drive home is quiet, and depressing. I begin to concede the need to change. Sylvia Ashton-Warner (1963) speaks of an "event" that triggers change. Could the hated lads be my event? Is Charles my catalyst? What does it all mean for me now? Will I have to sidestep administrative priorities to seek a new adventure? How am I to do that? I want to try something new. Where will this road lead? I must try to penetrate that antischool culture defended so well by the lads. I must learn to listen to them.

Friday is the first day of the new quarter. Tired from the previous evening of parent conferences, I walk into the first-period class with the same faces and the same atmosphere. But now I'm looking to my own educational reform.

The outside of November's chill permeates the classroom. I await the lads' reactions to their grades with a curiosity tainted with the hope that they will be stung, my moment of control. The lads' lethargic chatter suggests they did have a small effect, but now I will test my own control systems.

Charles enters, casual, indifferent, in power. I make my move.

"Charles, can I have a moment with you?" I say reservedly.

He sits down by my desk, curious.

"I know I've been a son-of-a-bitch to you this whole quarter. I want to start over." I am terse, tense, and earnest.

"I know I haven't made it any easier on you too. I'm willing to try," he matches my manner. He has no fear in his eyes. His decision is fast, like his decisions made daily on the streets. An offer of cooperation shows in his face. But I sense a Charles whose strength I still have not fully grasped. No student, I feel, in all my years of teaching, has had such a grip on life as this one. The uneasy conversation ends. I reach out my hand to shake his, with hope for a new beginning. Odd that after 17 years of teaching I am challenged to change by a 17-year-old. Charles goes to the seat the lads have kept for him. I turn to face the curious stares and chatter of the class.

"Would you break up into small groups?" I quickly and nervously ask. "You can sit with whomever you like."

This is new. Everyone scrambles. Chairs screech, driven like bumper cars, pushed like baby carriages. Individual voices drown in cacophony. Five groups emerge. One is the lads. In my anxiety, I fill the void. I grab points of grammar from the chapter and assign a task to each group. Cries of abandonment erupt as I leave them to their tasks:

"We don't know how to do this stuff."

Confusion reigns, but I ignore it. "I'll be back," I assure them half-heartedly. I'm buying time. I place myself in the lads' circle, an unwanted guest in a sea of estrangement. I've not given them a task. They look at each other in irritation. Shaid puts his best foot forward.

"Why are you putting us in groups?"

How do I tell the lads the truth? That I can't control them. That I am frustrated. They know. "I need your help." I feel I sound false.

"We need you too," says Shaid, trying to smooth over the conflict. His reply also sounds hollow. He normally avoids confrontation. I feel awkward.

"You don't really need us," Erick pushes. He measures his every word as he measures mine. I knew I'd hear from him. Erick is hardened by anger and mistrust. He flares fast and fiercely. He is not one I'd confront casually. His eyes speak: "What's this white man saying he needs us?"

I feel I am sinking into a lie. I try to shed it. I sidestep Erick.

"I know learning French doesn't mean anything to you guys. But there is work to be done. You can talk about anything you need to talk about. We're going to be here together for 7 more months." I don't know what more to say. I stumble out with, "When you're ready to join the large group, you can join us." I try to acknowledge my failure and their resistance while giving them a choice, even an invitation to join and work. Instead, I make them feel they are the outsiders, wrong if they don't join the rest. I am still pushing French on them. My old self speaks while I try to find my new voice. The dilemma is not resolved. I'm not making it.

Tough, cynical Erick presses, "I don't like the way you order us around."

"Then why don't you cooperate," I counter defensively. "You guys come in here unprepared, no book, no paper, no nothing." I angrily rattle off admonitions. The defiant stare back. It's not working. I reign myself.

"I hate grammar," says Aaron with true feeling.

"I know, it gets boring. But, Aaron, you don't even try; you're in the washroom more than you're in class." More admonitions. His head goes back, eyes rolling in frustration. I'm losing them quickly. I must stop this. "Look you guys, this stuff isn't hard. I'll help you get through it. We've got a long way to go 'til June. I know it doesn't mean shit to you, but we've got to go on. I'll try to make your lives in here more bearable. If you need to talk about anything, go ahead; but let me know. Let's see if we can work together." I am talking from my heart now. This is better. It begins to show. They're all staring hard at me—glued.

I glance at Charles, sensing his piercing, evaluating silence. I see the lads beginning to feel my frustration and my attempt to change. Again I am short for words, a stranger in their presence. Nervousness grips me. I've got to get away from them. They need their time. I escape to the others. Now the ball is in their hands. It's in mine too. But will it bring a new ball game?

The bell rings. Relief! Students wrestle out of their chairs and hustle to the exit. The chatter is intense. As Charles passes, he extends his hand to shake mine.

"Good-bye, Mr. Colsant." It is the first time all year that he has greeted me.

"Good-bye, Charles."

With all of them gone I pick up my blue book bag, stare at the empty chairs, drained, worried, unsure but hopeful.

DIFFERENT VOICES

For the next few days, I'm not at all sure where this change is taking my curriculum. In all my years of teaching I've never had this uneasy feeling. The class is loose, too loose for me. But it is a start. The brief conversation with Charles begins a ripple of change. A new order is in the making. It is nebulous, but destined to incorporate them. Their presence, their world—which I had ignored—smashes into my world. Their voices are to speak as much as my French curriculum. I must accept this and go on.

The days begin to pass more quickly. The classroom chill of November slowly departs. The new effort of collaboration is paying off. Though I'm tense, this lessens. They are accepting me more, but now it is on more mutual terms. I observe the class closely. They are working relatively well. I feel less need to be the source of control. Almost everyone talks while they work. They are comfortable with that; I'm not. But it allows me to see their individual personalities. A feeling of warmth toward the class grows.

Lisa, dark black bangs, red lips, walks in late. She must hold the school's record for tardiness. I'm supposed to collect tardy slips and note them in my record book, but I nod for her to put it in the trash. Her late entrance distracts the class. She acknowledges this without my prompting.

"Mr. Colsant," she volunteers, "I promise to be more on time."

I'm grateful for the attempted change of heart. Small miracles are just fine. She discards the tardy slip and I gain a student who promises to arrive on time. Lisa joins one of the small groups working on translations.

I notice that the lads feel incompetent at this task. Some split up and drift into other groups where they know they'll have greater access to answers. But I must be fair; some lads show a newer desire to understand. Three lads, Charles, Dion, and William, connect with Rachel. Still feeling like the outsider, I join them. I know Rachel has accepted me, so I take advantage of that. I enter their conversation, cautiously.

"Is everything going okay?"

William looks up with a lost nod and half grin. He feels slow with French, but has social clout. Right now his attention is on Rachel.

"Come on over closer, baby. You know what I mean," he boasts while he makes his mild attempts at work. I let his comment pass.

"Forgit ch'ou, William." She doesn't let it pass. William creates local theater. He's more interested in that than in French. The ears of the class are alert for his quick humor. They almost count on it. Accepting it is another adjustment for me. In fact, I'm enjoying what I tried to squash before. Encouraged somewhat by their collaborative work, I leave them. Low-keyed conversations continue to pop up. I move about, mingling in other groups.

"Look, man, this ain't hard."

It's Charles's voice. I look back. His head is in the book. He's trying to do his part. He seems different. He's almost enjoying the task.

"I'm gettin' it," he says.

I return to my desk. Papers start coming in. Students are at my desk. I move back to theirs. The aloneness of teaching ebbs.

I hear gang-bang talk from some of the other lads. This open "unruliness" doesn't bother them, but it bothers me. I can't adjust to the change as quickly as they can. Sometimes, I see slippage in what I consider the proper amount of work, the "necessary" chapters to be covered. So I get pushy. If I confront Janelle, she retreats from her work. If I confront Stephanie, she goes into a foul mood. Then there is Marcus: quick and eager to work, but eager-to-be-noticed Marcus. He'll start bugging me for "bugging's sake." He wants everything he does checked out immediately. He does little on his own. If I push work, he'll push verification. He drives me crazy. He has to have everything checked out step-by-step to proceed.

"Is this right, Mr. Colsant? Is this right?" he yells out. "Is this right?"

"Marcus, can't you see I'm ignoring you? Can't you think?"

"You're the teacher," he throws in my face; "you're supposed to be helping me."

"I'm no private tutor; you're supposed to think." I get frustrated with their incessant needs or questions that they can answer themselves. The quiet I used to maintain sometimes seems an attractive shield. But McNeil's thoughts on defensive, controlling, manipulative teaching re-enter my mind. I know I can't go back. I have to slow down; I have to just be with them. They are at peace and progressing comfortably. Their jovial bantering and caring mesh together. They're not excluding me or my French. It's their twist on learning, and I have to accept it. In truth the class is doing fine. Relax.

It's December, complete with snow flurries. There is a contented, working buzz in the room. In walks Mr. Brach of the business department pushing the sale of candy for the seniors' outgoing gift to the school. His committee wants to install a new marquee in front of the building. "Really," I think, "it's the committee's own attempt at immortality." I'm taking on the lads' cynicism.

"Can I ask the class how they're coming on the sale of candy?" he asks loudly so everyone can hear. What am I supposed to say? "No, get out." Irritated, I acquiesce. Our school abounds with interruptions.

"Has anybody sold any candy yet for the seniors' gift to the school?" he asks.

No one bothers to answer.

"Do you need some time to think about it?"

No answers. Just dull expressions.

"Alright, I'll give you more time to sell. You can give it to anybody at work, at church, anywhere."

"Gee, thanks, Mr. Brach," I think. "That's kind of you." I want him to leave, but he lingers. Dion, a tall, robust, handsome lad pipes up at the word "church."

"I haven't been to church in a long time," he confesses, changing the subject.

The class maintains its quiet in the face of Mr. Brach's questioning.

He senses their disinterest and becomes nervous. The students in turn work on, heads down, hoping he'll disappear.

"Well, I guess you just need more time," he breaks in with resignation.

"Yah, that's it," Aaron yells out. "We need more time." Mr. Brach bids them good-bye but promises to return. The door closes. The class takes up Dion's topic of church. It absorbs them. They seem happy.

SOME DOUBTS

The days themselves are now beginning to have their own personalities. I begin to know what to expect for the day. It's like I'm feeling their pulse, anticipating, whom not to bug, whom to tease; letting the personalities develop rather than trying to straitjacket them. The lads are often spread throughout the class. Today, however, they are all off in the corner. Not one has a book. I decide to circulate, but they beat me to it. Their conversation comes to a smooth end. They begin to join those who are well into the lesson. I guess I'm still the teacher, the outsider.

"How are you doing Dion?" I ask hinting at class work, knowing full well he can't explain a thing. Conciliatory Shaid answers for Dion.

"I'm really liking this stuff." He coats over their secretive meeting.

"Yah, right," I think quietly to myself. But I remember I promised them their own time.

Shaid, also forgetting that promise, says, "Seriously, I can say bonjour, mama."

"God," I think, "my nebulous curriculum, my nonpushy curriculum; where is this all going for them?"

Tralon, a very isolated lad, shakes my hand. I interpret this as a substitute for work or a sign that my time is up with them. But maybe it's just a gesture of good will? I still push to find out what the lads are up to. From across the room Earle gratuitously intervenes, beating rhythm on his desk.

"Hey, music boy," someone calls. The class laughs.

"Hey man! Hey music box!"

"What's going on in your head, Earle?" I ask.

"I'm meditating," he calmly replies.

"Why doesn't he discipline himself to stay with the others?" I think. Is that my old self? I back off. What is wrong with a moment of meditation? He is alive in it.

"I play drums for my church," Earle says proudly.

Maybe, I hope to myself, he'll join us in our curriculum. At the end of class Earle stops to talk. His parents have kicked him out of the house, so he stays with his grandmother. He did have something to meditate. He is as adrift in my class as he is outside. How many times in the past have I stopped students from revealing their lives? Now the toil of listening begins to weigh on me. Their unique stories deepen my understanding, enrich my own world. I never did get to the bottom of the lads' clandestine meeting. Their clever exclusion works, but there is no animosity.

Our learning continues. The next day, I notice that Naim, who is good natured and resilient, has an earring in each ear. There are big bold signs posted on the corridor walls "No Earrings or Hats on Men Are Allowed." My old self grabs me. I call out, reinforcing the rules, perhaps taking advantage of his sensitive nature.

"Naim, take off those earrings, now! You know the school rules. They look goofy, anyway." He obeys.

I see Charles's head pop up. I feel my authoritarian "now" course through his body. He hates that in me. Erick's November salvo of hatred for my authoritarian ways flashes through my mind. How I feel the chill return to the room! Why didn't I say it differently? It's hard to discard old baggage.

It is early December. The class is under way. In walks Charles, dead late. "Are we having a test today?"

He's using a lad tactic on me, skirting his tardiness. With the school's new rule, I'm supposed to send him for a tardy slip. Several tardies equal detention. The room is suddenly tense. They wait my reaction.

"Damn," I feel. "He's putting me through one of his tests. Ease up."

"No, test is tomorrow," I say curtly. "Go ahead, Charles, have a seat."

The class silently approves. Am I abdicating responsibility? Is this the risky part of side-stepping the administration? Is he controlling? Is there room for understanding? All turn back to work, and Charles joins in. My warm feeling toward the class returns.

Dion, the humorist, is giving someone the finger from across the room. I let it go. If it happens again, we'll talk. Those little annoyances still bug me.

Erick approaches my desk. He tells me that Cherrie's mother died of a heart attack back in October. Though he and Cherrie are the same age, she is his auntie, and they sit together in my class. Why tell me now, in December? I see Cherrie's head on her desk. Why wasn't I told by any of the counselors? No wonder she's so indifferent and defensive. She never said a word. Erick never said a word. Probably because he couldn't stand me the first quarter. Now he tells me. Is the ice cracking here too? Cherrie's head remains cushioned on her arms as I glance, wondering.

The bell interrupts. Eyes shift to the clock. Their test is tomorrow. It weighs on me. It's their first attempt at traditional "success" since the disastrous first quarter.

"Good luck on your test tomorrow. Get some studying done tonight. Review those exercises."

The teacher in me is speaking. I don't know if it's even heard. They just expect me to say it. The class finishes on a positive note. Four free minutes until the next class.

Test day comes fast. There's extra-loud chatter—anxiety. The more talk, the better, they hope. Delay that test. Let confusion reign.

"Make sure your names and the class period are put on your answer sheet." Why do I say these stupid little reminders?

"What's the date?" someone calls out. It's a call for reassurance as much as for information. They settle in.

Three minutes into the test, I look up to watch Erick, right in front of me, randomly filling in the blanks. I guess my gut feeling that the lads want to learn doesn't apply to everyone. Is he giving me the "quid pro quo" of the first quarter?

Erick and Earle both stare off into space in quiet frustration. I interrupt Erick's daydreaming.

"Erick, do you want extra help?"

He agrees lethargically. The next day he passes the retake, but what does it mean? If there is satisfaction in teaching, it must lie in student-teacher collaboration rather than in test scores. I'm still failing with Erick and Earle.

It's December 6, the feast of St. Nicholas, the first day of the French Christmas season. A videocassette with the origin and tradition of this special holiday is set to go. Deron, a well-built 5-foot-7-inch wrestler for the school, comes in angry. He stalks to his desk, bangs his books down and peers out the window. His classmates are entering.

"What's the matter, Deron?"

"She [the new principal] don't give a damn. She's taken away our wrestling room and now she's added these stupid tardies; she's moving too fast for me. She don't give a damn about our wrestling team. And now these stupid tardies with detentions and in-house suspensions. It don't make sense." When Deron is angry it's because things "don't make sense."

Others are upset too. Karin has a long face. The bell rings. Keesha strides in even faster than Deron.

"You can't get from one end of the building to the other in four minutes," Keesha rumbles, her eyes staring off at an angle.

"Why don't you carry two sets of books," I suggest omnisciently.

"Because I just come from the gym," snaps Deron. "And they'll steal 'em from the lockers."

He's right. The whole class attacks the complex tangle of problems created by the new tardy rules and the ever-present threat of theft. Well, not the whole class. After 15 minutes of wrangling, Brigitte cuts in, "I think we should be getting back to French."

"I think Deron's anger is legitimate and he's got a right to express it," I shoot back irritated.

The class is encouraged to confront Brigitte further. But I'm thinking I should have let them confront her bravery. I think of my control systems. It's not just our use of school knowledge to control and administrative obsession with order that undermines us; it's our inability to listen to student anger and student hope. I regret my challenge to Brigitte. Christmas's entry with the feast of St. Nicholas doesn't turn out as I planned. I discard my lesson plans. The period ends with us all more frustrated and uneasy.

The following day Brigitte comes to me before class.

"Mr. Colsant, can I speak to the class?"

"Is it about yesterday?"

"Yes," she nodded.

"Do you feel it's necessary? I think the issue is over."

The bell interrupts; everyone gradually moves to their seats. The class grows silent more quickly as they observe Brigitte still standing and facing them. She clings to her desk for support.

"I want to ask for your forgiveness," she says humbly. "Yesterday, I just assumed that you wanted to waste time discussing tardies. I want to ask for your forgiveness," she repeats.

Asking forgiveness for assuming people wanted to goof off—that their concerns were not legitimate! A student publicly apologizes for wanting to get on with schoolwork—for letting her simple desire obscure the concerns of others. This is an apology I could have made countless times. Her open act of humility—her second act of courage—stuns us. The silence is crystalline. I thank Brigitte, groping for appropriate words. We resume our work, but with an embarrassed hurry. Brigitte has healed the previous day's hurt. She helped us to hear one another.

Breaking the silence, Deron announces, "I got accepted at Northern Illinois University." He got a wrestling scholarship. Questions pop up like the wild, red poppies of France.

Clare, one of the brighter students, softly states, "I'm not going to college. I don't think I'm college material, Mr. Colsant."

"Why's that, Clare?"

"I'm better at taking notes," she replies. "I want to be a secretary."

Willis's (1977) question of how working-class kids get working-class jobs comes to me. I'll have to get back to Clare. She could have messages to dictate as well as the skill to take dictation.

Christmas vacation looms. The days move faster. It's time to pull out the Yuletide carols tucked away in jam-filled cabinet folders. I love the French carols, but teaching them can be uncomfortable. It will be the first time they hear me sing: songs like "Bring Your Torch, Jeannette Isabelle," and "O Holy Night." I start with the beautiful French version of "O Holy Night." I pass out the song sheets and, then, while explaining a translation of the French version, I casually slip to the back of the room. There, the phenomenon of my singing won't be seen, just heard. It's me and the song sheet, a cappella. But heads all turn and I wind up in front of their staring, laughing faces. It's crazy, but I go through this performance every year. They oooh and aaah. But I persist with hope that if they hear these carols during the vacation, it will bring new meaning to Christmas and perhaps the rest of their lives.

THE RETURN

If Christmas came quickly, vacation went even more quickly. I am back with everyone, lads and all. I've got to restart. It's frightful. Courage. I have a consolation. I no longer dread the first period.

In they come, in high spirits. The lads are together again in the back. It seems only yesterday I was teaching them carols.

"How did your vacations go?"

They are alive with chatter about dinners, parties, movies, fun times—their winter curriculum. I scan the room. Charles has his head down on the desk. He's tracing red pen marks over his book.

"I've got to get based," I overhear him say. There is something wrong. My attention turns back to the class.

"Did anyone hear any of the French Christmas carols I taught you?"

To my surprise, Charles picks up his head and speaks out proudly, "We don't celebrate Christmas; we celebrate Kwanzaa" (an African-American celebration of life that starts the day after Christmas).

"Well, what is that like, Charles?"

"I'm just jerking your chain, Mr. Colsant." He puts his head back down, and the class has a good laugh on me. I have a taste of the bad old days. Is it just lad humor? Is he needing to reestablish peer leadership? Am I an equal in his joking? Still the outsider? I am reminded of my naiveté and absorb his comment with a grin.

The start back to work during the second week is sluggish. Shaid greets Charles with "What's up?" from clear across the room. Again, Charles's head is on his desk. Dion is talking about the Mideast crisis. The bombing has started on Iraq.

"Are you guys having a hard time getting to work?" I ask.

"I want to fight for my family," Dion seizes the moment.

"We don't belong over there," Shaid challenges. "I don't want to fight for some Arabs. This is Bush's war."

"What war are you talking about?" asks Olivia naively.

"Girl! Where have you been?" calls Sharon.

"They shouldn't have started the bombing on Martin Luther King Day," Rachel lands her own bomb. The conversation boils. Are they blowing a period? Are they involved? I'm not sure. The conversation is fast. Most students stay out but listen quietly while the debate whirls around them. I stay out too, wondering where it will go. Dion becomes less impassioned. The discussion runs its short course. Calm comes. Work continues.

My quandary about Dion's opening salvo lingers. I circulate round the room and to his desk. If the truth be known, he has no interest in French grammar. His urge to fight for family is there alright, but the Mideast crisis is his tool to sidetrack us. Rachel pinpoints a real disappointment. I can go on knowing that the digression was just that for some, yet the real curriculum for others. Now they are back to my curriculum. There are days of ambivalence. I'm getting there. I can live with that. Progress occurs on both sides. The divide between us is smaller.

The next day everyone walks in on time. Unusual! The principal had suggested that if someone enters late teachers casually step over to their desk while teaching and insert a slash in their record book. That way, the flow of teaching would not be interrupted. But long ago I chose forgetting the record book as the easiest way to prevent interruptions.

The public address system interrupts for some important words. It's the principal. The class proceeds. So does she. "The new tardy system is working," she announces. "Keep up the good work. And have a good day." A little politicking by the administration?

Erick has returned after a long "illness."

"Is there anything I can do to pass?" he asks in earnest.

"Yes, Erick." My old self feels like telling him he can go back to September and start with "bonjour." But he's in earnest and talking to a "different" teacher.

"I can give you some time, but it would be good to join your auntie in working together." I realize I've used the black pronunciation of "auntie" for the first time. It came naturally. I suppose I'm still changing. The strange becomes familiar as I listen and hear.

Earle approaches. "Can you lend me a dollar, Mr. C.?" This could embarrass us both. I reach for my wallet and hand over a dollar. We both manage to act as if he's asking for a piece of paper to write on.

Chandra is singing "rejoice, rejoice." I don't know why; I don't even care why. I'm just happy she's singing. The class is working on the reflexive verb *se coucher* (to go to bed). I decide to draw on how the absence of parents prevents children from being able to sleep; how a babysitter is no substitute for a mother's own security. The class reminisces silently, each one recalling memories evoking stories. I look out onto faces. They recollect quickly. Memories push their pens, testing their creativity as writers.

Stephanie has her head down on the desk. She's sick. Aaron is out of his desk. He is walking around the room again, blowing time. He approaches my desk. I anticipate, and hand him the hall pass.

"Here, Aaron, blow some more time."

The class joins me and laughs. They know I'm displeased, but not about to impose anything. I close out the period introducing the song, "Frere Jacques," with *dormir* (to sleep) to reinforce the verb *se coucher*. Once again, I maneuver to the back of the room. There, I start my solo with a bit more bravery. This time, they quickly turn it into a chorus.

Next day. Dion, inclusive jokester, springs to life.

"What's up, old Earle; why don't you come join us working?" he summons.

I am thinking I cannot interest Earle in French. He only likes to get me to digress. No textbook! That's it for Earle. Or is it? But here is Dion trying to draw him in.

In January, the memory of Martin Luther King, Jr., is alive in the building. At a special assembly, a student will read King's "I Have a Dream" speech. The administration usually invites a guest speaker who marched with King to rekindle his dream. It brings back my own memories when I heard him speak as a first-year college student in Washington, D.C., mingling in the crowd, not fully conscious of the grandeur of the occasion. I watched King with detached curiosity. King begins to mean more to me as I learn to see the "content of the characters" arrayed before me.

A conversation circulates the room about his legacy.

"He didn't do nothin' for me," Earle blurts out.

Not even King gets a green light from "old Earle," as the lads now call him. Why did the program office put Earle in French? Maybe he is here for me. Maybe it's my turn to be the learner.

Next day, the principal is on the P.A. system at 7:44 A.M., again encouraging students to be on time. "You have a few seconds to get to class."

There are more discipline problems in the halls and more late arrivals. The efficient tardy system is taking a nose dive.

The bell rings. Class begins. It is now 7:47. Again the intercom blurts. "This is Mrs. Lambert."

"We know," yells my class—all here on time.

"The tardy system is still working well," says the principal's voice. "Keep up the good work."

THE EXIT

Winter has long had its bitter grip on us. A robin's nest high outside our third-floor window is barren against the cold, blue sky. Inside, the classroom is more alive than ever. Things are moving well. The unanticipated occurs. Charles comes in toward the end of first period and hands me a yellow card to sign—the official student transfer card. I look at him stunned. I ask the obvious, "You're leaving?" He explains briefly. Family problems. The scene during the first two days after the Christmas break flashes back—his head down on two separate days should have been a tip-off. I should have known. I sign the card stumbling for words.

"I feel sorry you're leaving."

"Don't feel sorry for me," he answers.

He didn't receive the message I tried to send.

"No, Charles, I feel sorry you're leaving," I say dolefully.

He nods. I am already experiencing loss, not because of the curriculum experiment, but because of the person. This is the first time in my years of teaching that I am actually going to miss a student—this lad.

The next day Charles unexpectedly returns to go over with me some advice his counselor had given him. I am glad he seeks my advice, but I too see no alternative. It seems he must go—personal problems dictate a new school district. With adult composure, he shakes my hand for the third and last time, says good-bye and leaves. A quick, silent departure. The lads already knew he was leaving.

Charles's strength prodded me to realize that I had to see students differently. I see no reversal of this trend. I am committed. To think that I could only "control the class when [I] can control the street corner youngster" (Foster, 1986, p. 261) by showing him I am the Alpha wolf now seems ludicrous. Instead, I see Charles's contribution of bringing the inconsequential study of a romance language alive, to the lads and to the whole class. He woke me up to them. I did not need, as some suggest, to play a psych game or act in a "'crazy' way" to defeat "the street corner youngster's game of attempting to manipulate the class to his own ends" (Foster, p. 261).

The groups that had formed in late November have changed many times. Each group in its own way has contributed to the learning. Since Charles's departure, no equivalent leader has emerged. The lads still clan together, but not as strongly. They venture to other, more academically oriented groups. Dion in particular does this. He's restless but he gets work done. Aaron and Earle are still aimless, lost souls. I can't do a damn thing for them. The system has cursed them. Still, I include them with the many, creating curriculum here and there with what energy I have, and with what they can bring. Now, it's a rich exchange about and around French. I struggle to shape my teaching of French around their personalities and priorities. These are multitude.

The second quarter is ending. Students usually dismiss the first quarter as the "one that doesn't count." Now, all of a sudden, they're serious. "This period really counts." These grades are permanent. Dread time is here for teachers and students. In my class we are readying for the last major test before final exams. Infantile, anxious questions abound.

"Do you have a pencil?"

"Can I sharpen my pencil?"

"How long is this test?"

"Are there many questions?"

"Can I go to the washroom real quick?"

I give them my pep talk. The class finally settles into the test. I'm at my desk with busywork, correcting papers, answering notes, filing pamphlets. I notice two lads "sharing answers." I interrupt to give one of my rehearsed lectures on integrity versus cheating. They buy it, so it seems. In walks Marcus. He's been consistently coming late.

"Do you have a pencil for me?" he asks commandingly, as if I'm supposed to have one. Student heads go up. Testing halts. My quiet goes. With a rush of anger I blurt out, "That is your responsibility. No, I don't have one! It's just too damn bad!"

A roar of laughter goes up. They know Marcus has it coming.

"It's just too damn bad," William mimics with a wide grin. "Colsant's snapping. That's the first time Colsant's snapped."

William defuses my anger and saves Marcus and me. The old ever-snapping Colsant is but a memory to be joked about. I resume correcting papers. The test continues. All is well.

Midway through the test, Shaid collapses.

"I can't do this for a long time." He puts his head down. There's a chain reaction. Aaron suddenly has to visit the washroom, as if to defend Shaid's frustration. Earle starts his drum roll, hitting the desk with gentle taps. I motion to stop.

"Thank you, Earle."

He stops. Attention returns to the test until it ends. The students leave calmly, relieved it's over.

A few class periods later, I see Dion in the library between the stacks talking with his girl friend.

"Hi, Mr. Colsant," he cracks. "A little French going on." That's a generous interpretation of our curriculum.

The next day Dion is the first to enter class. I read "Oh, no; not me" on his face. He turns to exit.

"Be brave, Dion," I kid him. "Be the first to stay in." He moves quickly to his desk, flips his books down and heads back toward the door. It's too late. Cherrie's entering.

"Dion's first in class," she sings.

"Don't have to be second all the time in life," he quips defensively. The others drift in, in good spirits.

"Quelle heure est-il?" asks Rachel in good French.

"My God," I think! "There's actual French being used—spontane-ously." The class is noisy. Bell rings. The loud chatter drowns out the announcements over the P.A. system.

"Shut up and listen," Tonia shouts out with her autocratic tone. Everyone shuts up. Well, that was easy, I think. Lisa again walks in late and goes up the aisle.

"Boy, I'd like to dance around your mulberry bush," Dion comments as she passes.

Erick comes alive. This is curriculum for him.

"You know what he means, Mr. Colsant?"

"Ya, Erick. I get the picture. Dion, can I see you after class?"

"Oooooh Dion," the class calls in unison, half-joking! They know this doesn't mean confrontation as it would have before, but they also ex-pect me to do some form of "formal" admonishing.

With midterm exams over, grades must be given. I decide to try something I've never done. They will give themselves their semester grade. They already know their exam grade. They know what effort they've made and the results of past tests. So, it seems to me they know where they stand in terms of an overall grade.

"Would you all take out a sheet of paper?" I ask. "Put your names on them." There is a nervous scurry.

"What's up?" I hear in various renditions.

"I'd like you to put your heads on your desks, close your eyes, and go deep into yourselves." There are some fearful resisters. Most heads go down. Eventually all.

"Imagine you are finishing your studies abroad; you are alone in the French Alps. There is just you and the surrounding beauty of the mountains. What you see is nature's truth. The beauty you are surrounded with is all true. You have just finished your short stint in learning French. You know how much effort you have given to this adventure. Now, alone on this mountain top, all alone, search your interior and give yourself a grade. Stay within yourself, give yourself a grade and justify it." My hope is to bring them more into collaboration, to face the process of evaluation, and avoid dividing them from me by assigning grades. They are left to confront the truth or the lie.

Quietness reigns. It's still-life. Then heads begin to perk up. Pens and pencils move. Papers are passed in. Of the 24 who submitted a grade with its justification, I disagreed with only two students, who I thought inflated their grades and whose justifications also seemed inflated. Others were too harsh, and I pushed them up. I held private conferences with the two. We discussed what I thought were inconsistencies, and a new grade was agreed on.

Near the end of February, good-natured Naim comes into the room unexpectedly early. I initiate the conversation I suspect he wants.

"Yesterday, I saw your name on the 'wanted list.'" That's my term for "detainees" in in-school suspension. It's the system's way of expelling the student from the classroom but not from the school, thus no loss of state money.

"I didn't serve my detention," he answered.

I ask why.

"Because I didn't deserve it; I walked out on Mr. Anderson [dean of discipline] because he didn't want to hear what I had to say."

"What was that?"

"You don't want to hear it," he countered. I feel he means "I want to tell the story, but I'll be embarrassed telling it."

"Try me."

"We was playing cards at my uncle's house," he starts, "and we receive a phone call from my cousin. She say her baby is upstairs in the closet. So we rush up to the place and we find the baby strangled to death. I freaked out."

The drilling sound of the corridor bell and the adolescent chatter bursting into the classroom interrupts our conversation. Naim's story needed closure. It had none. The only real closure I could offer him at that moment was a communicative silence. I experience anew what it means to quietly listen.

Isn't it, I think, through the art of listening to every Charles, Clare, and Naim that the doors to education are opened? The stories of teenagers seem wholly unique. And they are; but in a way they're the same. They're the same story told differently—about adolescents who eternally confront the system, or authoritarian figures, nonlistening teachers, and administrative dictates, the intercom that never hears.

The dean of discipline who sent Naim to a day of in-school suspension will never realize that. Since that late November Friday when I held the brief conversation with Charles to this day of mid-June, I have not sent a single student to his office. He will never know that that brief conversation with Charles began a wider conversation with all the others; that of the 1,029 parent conferences the dean boasted of having completed this year, not one of them since that Friday was mine. That forever will be a comfort to me, a tribute to that first-period class—a silent tribute to the "event" whose name is Charles, a lad long since gone, who challenged me to listen, to receive as well as give.

Without Charles, there would have still been my voice crying in the wilderness, delivering my sacred messages to a small priesthood and a captive, alienated congregation. No longer is my class divided into a chosen few and the many. Now, if there is a few it is those I still cannot reach or draw into the conversation.

NEW VOICES

"Who's the Secretary of State?" asks Chandra.

"Jim Edgar" someone shouts.

"No he's not. He's the new governor."

Tonia turns to Dion, "Veux-tu manger du pain?"

I'm floored; it's in good French.

Dion proudly responds "oui" but massacres the rest of his response. Embarrassed, he's quick to bolster his own genre of French. "I'm going to tutor Janelle—tonight."

But he reads my face and seeks more honesty.

"I tried."

"I did too, Dion," I answer, matching his honesty.

The following day is an off-day for me. Perhaps I'm just tired. I'm talking to the class about too many unnecessary distractions. I dig out one of my old-style lectures.

"You all have to quiet down; there's too much talking going on." I "hear" McNeil (1986) at the door. I know what I'm doing now with that admonition. Student work continues. I enjoy the quiet respite. God must be on my side. Or so I think. Out of nowhere, two fire engines, sirens blasting, roll around the southeast corner of the school and stop under our windows. Students stampede to the windows.

"It's the house across the street," someone calls.

William gleefully challenges a few laggards. Up they go. I surrender to their moment. I join them at the "lookout." It was a false alarm. They return to work grateful for the entertainment. They did it their way.

Out of nowhere: "Fuck you, bitch."

"Oooooh Olivia" in rising crescendo goes the class.

"Sorry, Mr. Colsant," Olivia says grinning.

I have no idea what the problem is. Olivia puts her head down, yet somehow she's relishing the attention. Work proceeds.

It's now early spring. Chandra, Tonia, Olivia, and Sharon, who individually have been almost invisible, emerge as a cohesive presence. They have grown closer. I watch them, curious to know what will evolve. They work together and pretty much stay to themselves. Tonia, however, is the most outgoing of the four. Their impact on the class does not match that of the lads, but in the new climate they feel freer to express themselves. I sense no threat from this gregarious foursome. They're in constant chatter. Earlier, I would have stopped it, but they do it while they work. Sometimes it does drive me crazy, but we talk about when chatter is okay, and they promise politeness and cooperation when I need those moments for class instruction. I openly call them "my grandmas." So does the class. Tonia occasionally sings in class. Her latest song is the old tune "Mr. Sandman."

Today, Chandra has no book.

"Can I have a book, Mr. Colsant? I'm very tired and couldn't get to my locker," she says.

I'm not sympathetic. I normally charge 25 cents to encourage book-bringing.

"Yah, right."

But Tonia, sympathetic to Chandra's plight, breaks out in song with her new sandman lyrics, "Mr. Colsant, bring me a book." I give in, charmed by her ingenuity. Again, work proceeds where there would have been hostility.

Today, I announce the results of a recent major test. Students are anxious, but the news is good. They come up privately to see their grades. They prefer it that way. It lessens embarrassment and yet adds suspense. Up comes Shaid. One glance into my record book and he announces his B, taking several bows. He turns to me.

"I really want to thank you. I'm learning French. I want to thank my mother and father. I'm drinking more milk for my brain." The class cheers, whistles. Shaid adds more bows and returns triumphantly up the aisle to his seat waving his clasped hands.

Sharon is next. She peeps frighteningly in my book and openly screams, "I got a B." I've made her day. More truly, she's made her own day and I can share in it. That's a celebration of life right there.

The next day I started class with the music to the record "Tour de France." Drawn in by the musical panting of the bicyclist, Tonia dances into the room, interpreting the panting with the rhythmic flow of her body. Others join.

"Let's sing to it," says Dion. The shyer ones settle for work, but they enjoy the performances. Too early, the record spins to its end.

Sensitive Naim is up at the board. He calls me "chief" now. Each group chooses a spokesperson to teach the whole class the pooled efforts of their assigned task. Naim is chosen today. I ask students to challenge him if they prefer their own explanations or want to add to his. Little does Naim know—it's a setup; I assigned the same task to another group. Debate is heated on a simple point of grammar. It's crazy. One day grammar is completely out of the question; today it's a challenge. Follow-up exercises are next. I scan the room. Erick is off to the side. He's like Earle. They're both in a boxing ring swinging, but getting their heads bashed. It's a dead end for both.

"What's wrong, Erick?" There's no work.

"I don't know; I just didn't start on it." He's staring at the page.

"Isn't it clear?" I'm not challenging him.

"Ya, I'm fittin' to do it now."

Earle is against the wall with his head down. Is he sick? Lord, who knows?

Clare just told me she's changed her mind about not going to college. She no longer wants to take notes. She's decided to go to Roosevelt University. I congratulate her. Clare is now unwilling to let herself be condemned to a life of doing the bidding of others.

It is now mid-May. Warm. A long way from the hostile days of November. A student just plunked copies of the school newspaper on my desk. I scan the "who's who" section. My eyes pop. Dion has been named "Most Popular of the Senior Class." Dion? That can't be! The same Dion I have in my class? I'm off guard. I go back to my notes on the class. Why, in all the months since Charles's departure, hadn't I identified this new leader? How blind can I be? There he is, "Most Popular of the Senior Class of '91." How long it takes to hear and understand students. I am still processing them through "teacher-academic-eyes." Classroom subtleties go hidden. The personality of my classroom undergoes change after change. With all this change I miss the subtlety of Dion. Sylvia Ashton-

Warner's (1963) words resound, "But I'm so slow. You never saw anyone as slow as me when something is under my nose" (p. 139). I try to
understand the personality of each emerging group and the individual
that contributes to each. That endeavor alone needs vigilance and pa-
tience. Adolescents test out their subtle powers of resistance on us. Sometimes, they turn this power into a shield. Yet they want to feel I care.
They love closeness. It is a constant paradox to wrestle with. Most teachers and students survive this paradox; others succumb. We assume the
students are here to drink in our content knowledge. We pay scant attention to the real-life knowledge as it impacts school knowledge, made
so available for their betterment. We clap when the dean of discipline
proudly boasts of 1,029 parent-discipline conferences he has "effectively"
completed. We do not stop to think of the hidden correlation between
our school knowledge and these "effective" disciplinary conferences. We
know our subject; cognitive content is delivered. We have our agenda;
the legitimacy of the institution is secured. We have our paycheck. And
academia walks across the stage to receive its own self. The system kids
itself in a way. Reform? How do you put your finger on that elusive phenomenon? The classroom is the place. It has its own call, a journey trig-
gered by an event, a book, a defiant lad. The teacher listens to this event,
this call to reform. It becomes sequential as the flow of night into morning. Openness to this call brings one closer to the human being, deeper
into his or her mystery. It becomes our challenge. Each reform is a story.
But it resides in the toil of quiet listening. To be present to the students'
inconsequential chatter, their silence, their voice. It is to live the conversation, to walk not into the classroom but into the world of the students.

It's the first week of June. Graduation is here. The school is wild.
The seniors are running around yelling, "Seniors, Seniors." The juniors
get into the act countering, "Juniors, Juniors." The underclassmen stand
back in awe. Their yell has to wait.

"I like learning French," William says. "You inspire me. You should
be awarded teacher of the year." I thank William. Lisa came in late today.
Her grandfather died over the weekend. He was in his seventies. She was
close to him. She's very quiet.

Cherrie is back after a long absence. She's still under the melancholy
from her mother's death. I can't reach her. Erick is lost also. Did I fail
them? Did the system initiate their failure long ago? Did they fail themselves?

I look out onto the young audience. It remains young, filled with its
turmoil. But the teacher in me no longer feels like the agent of the system, bound to do it good despite its unwillingness, blindness, and resistance. Still in it, I let the system go to create a new system. My heart lies

more in what Paul Willis (1977) calls the "crucial relationship" between teacher and student, a sharing of the classroom. Teaching is becoming vigilant, empathic listening, free from coercion. The student then becomes a teacher; the teacher, a student. Our doing becomes our learning. I think that is reform. This is what I try. Perhaps, then, the once-felt, intense emotions of a September excitement can linger far longer than the thirtieth of that same month.

REFLECTIONS

Postscript 1: I met Dion's mother for the first time in September of the next year. It was Dion's funeral. He was shot. I felt out of place, but compelled to come—the only white person there. She thanked me for coming.

"Dion spoke of you," she said with sad and grateful acknowledgment.

I was deeply touched. She included me. A year ago, I would never have come.

Some say his death was gang related. Others have different stories. In any case, because he had graduated, our school is not in official mourning. But those of us who knew Dion are in mourning. Dion in the casket did not seem real. I could not approach him lying there. He was too young to be dead. He's just asleep. Three months ago, he was learning French and bringing life to my classroom: calling "old Earle" to learn, vowing to "tutor" Janelle, supporting his country against Iraq, "doing French" with his girl in the library stacks. Now he is dead, not here to share the life he helped bring to us. This chapter is for Dion and his mother, for without them it would not be whole.

Postscript 2: Two of my "grandmas" and two lads have chosen to come with me for this second year. Chandra's smile is pretty as ever. She challenges me quite openly and honestly when I don't follow up on a commitment to the class or she feels I've done her an injustice. She really sets the record straight and smiles victoriously when I concede error. Tonia, her hair up in a bun and flowing on out in curls, sits right close, eager to back her up. My world is good with them in it. They're still teaching me.

William, the dramatist, is twice as funny this year. I subtly encourage his local theater. He knows it, and runs with it.

And then there's Marcus. He doesn't bug me as much. He's adopted my catch phrase, "I don't know; think it through." He calls it out when others pester with questions they can probably answer, and I use it more freely. Now all my students recognize it. I have posted "I don't know;

think it through!" banners on our dull corridor walls. They tell me it's catching. I hope it will strengthen the Naims of the school in the face of the national achievement tests that dog us every year.

Postscript 3: Of Charles, I know only that he went to the west side of Chicago. I hope he has graduated. I see him in new students, but the "nigger he's gonna love to hate" is no more. New lads are there all right, not remote antagonists, but alive in the toil of listening. New conversations will surely emerge.

REFERENCES

Ashton-Warner, S. (1963). *Teacher*. New York: Touchstone/Simon and Schuster.

Foster, H. (1986). *Ribbin', jivin', and playin' the dozens: The persistent dilemma in our schools*. New York: Herbert L. Foster Associates.

McNeil, L. (1986). *Contradictions of control: School structure and school control*. New York: Routledge & Kegan Paul.

Willis, P. (1977). *Learning to labor: How working class kids get working class jobs*. New York: Columbia University Press.

5 Mathematics in the City

THE DESIRE FOR MEANING AND THE FEAR OF FREEDOM

Cathryn Busch, University of Illinois at Chicago

Students with Ada Harris (at rear) and Cathryn Busch

Bothered by the mathematics performance of the students in the inner-city school where she was principal, Cathryn Busch examined teachers' and students' purposes. These proved to be at odds with the notion that learning should be exciting. She and one of her teachers drew students into an attempt at change. Both teachers and students who want meaningful learning must, she and her collaborating teacher found, face the fear of freedom and adopt the mantle of those before them who sought their own meanings.

Working in my office, I did not hear the 2:30 dismissal bell. Only when I heard the junior high students pass my office to leave the building did I realize it was the end of the school day. I generally go outside to say good-bye as the students leave. Their faces beam and they show more vitality than at any other time of the day. I like to hope this is because they have had a productive enjoyable day in school with their friends and teachers.

"Good-bye, Mrs. Busch," a few called as they passed my office. I glanced up. "Good-bye, children." But they were gone before I could see them. I stepped into the hallway. A few seventh-grade boys running down the hall screeched to a halt as soon as they saw me, nearly tripping over each other. They waved good-bye, escaping before I could correct them.

I again checked the clock. "It could not possibly be 2:30," I thought. In fact, it was hard for me to believe that there were only a few weeks until summer vacation. The year had passed too quickly. This was the end of my sixth year as principal. Yet the thought that I was responsible for the education of nearly 300 children in kindergarten to grade 8 still overwhelmed me. So much remained to be done.

I had spent the majority of the afternoon at my desk working on the afternoon's faculty meeting agenda. We were to continue discussing plans for next year. In previous meetings we had discussed our standardized test scores. There were slight improvements in a few areas. Each year we devised new ways to help our students learn, but the task seemed to become more rather than less difficult.

In the faculty room, teachers helped themselves to refreshments while they shared their adventures of the day. There was an air of eagerness to get through the last few weeks of the year. If they were tired they did not show it. Nevertheless, remembering how draining the closing weeks of school can be, I promised not to keep them longer than necessary. We began with the first agenda item, my "assignment" from our last meeting—suggestions that might help us improve our math program for next year. I asked what materials they would suggest we purchase. Mr. Hall, the junior high math teacher, suggested some and a few others described materials that they wanted to try.

The optimistic tone changed when Mrs. Taylor, the sixth-grade teacher, interrupted, "I used that program myself. I thought it was pretty good. But you know, as I told Mrs. Busch many times this year, my difficulty is not with the materials. We have good math materials but so many of the kids are just not interested in learning anymore. I hate to sound so

This project was supported in part by the Center for Urban Educational Research and Development, University of Illinois at Chicago.

negative about them, but it's hard to get them involved in their work and the parents don't help."

The others joined in. Faith in new materials was suddenly replaced by pessimism about student motivation. Too many students are just not interested in learning anything. We were back to that old topic—students aren't interested in learning and parents don't care. Motivation was not an agenda item but it captures the meeting.

I understood the teachers' frustration. I felt for them and for the students. The children were my responsibility too. Six years ago when I became principal, armed with a Master's Degree in Educational Administration and eight years of teaching experience, I believed I had all the solutions. But that was then. It hit me that new materials would not be enough.

"You know it's not just us," Mrs. Walker added. "I have friends in other schools in the city who say it's just as bad. The children are not interested. It's a pain to get an assignment out of them. Some spend more time making excuses for not doing an assignment than doing the assignment itself."

Mr. Hall reluctantly nodded agreement with Mrs. Walker. I felt particularly bad for him. He had taught for 10 years in another city, then had a successful business career. He returned to teaching because he truly loved it. During his first year at our school he started a math club. He came an hour early to help students with special math projects. Student participation was low, yet he has maintained his energy for three years. If he gives up hope of motivating students what can I hope for? I had to find something to help my teachers. As I reflected on Mrs. Walker's comment, a distressing question entered my mind. Is this what teachers of urban African-American students must always face?

The longer the discussion went on the more it became obvious that what I had been asking the teachers to come up with was a "quick fix" to our problems. I could see that a bandage of materials and manipulatives would not work. We needed fresh ideas about student motivation.

This discussion stimulated me to embark on a journey into strategies for motivating students. I hoped later to use what I learned in my own school. Perhaps, I thought, other teachers who were faced with similar dilemmas could provide insight. I began by interviewing teachers during the summer, talking with my own the following year, and participating in a more detailed exploration. I wanted to find out how other teachers got their students involved in learning and to find out if they shared the belief that motivation was a major problem. I selected at random 10 inner-city schools and asked the principals for help. They gave me the names of their third- and fourth-grade teachers. I contacted each teacher by telephone. I felt fortunate that 8 of the 10 teachers agreed to talk with me—three white and five African-American women. I was excited about what I might learn.

TEACHERS' BELIEFS ABOUT MOTIVATION

My first interview was scheduled for late June. I met Marianne, a fourth-grade teacher and veteran of 28 years, at an outdoor cafe. We sat at a small table and I suggested we order something to eat. I was not the least bit hungry, but I felt that discussing the menu was a good icebreaker. We both ordered croissants and coffee, which we hardly touched. I wanted to understand Marianne, how she felt about being white and teaching African-American students in an inner-city school. I followed her eyes as she spoke. I could sense her sincere concern about her children, and I understood her feeling of helplessness. I had seen the look in her eyes many times before—in the eyes of many of my teachers. I had expected the interview to last less than an hour. The 120-minute tape turning off reminded me how long we had been sitting. I left the meeting with Marianne feeling exhausted.

As the summer months breezed away I continued my interviews. I was confident that every teacher I spoke with was comfortable and honest with me. They seemed relieved that someone was willing to seek their knowledge on an important issue.

Some common themes emerged in the transcripts. The most pronounced was that the teachers were very concerned about their students' self-esteem. They described strategies designed to build up the students' confidence in math.

Ella, for example, said, "I try to make them feel good about their math ability. Math is very hard for them. I don't tell them how many they have wrong, only how many they have right. If I put up papers, I don't put grades on them. Their self-esteem is very low. If they come to school and pay attention, they may have earned a D, but I give them a C. You don't want to tear them down."

Rita said, "If they see that the problems are hard or take too long, it's 'I'm not going to try.' I have to work on their self-esteem."

Seven of the eight teachers said that because of low self-esteem, students give up if a problem offers too much of a challenge. They also said they attempt to relate math concepts to everyday, real-world activities such as shopping at the grocery store and using money. As Sheri said, "I try to relate it to everyday life. They need these skills in order to deal with life, in order to go to the store and buy a bag of potato chips and a pop. If you're going to give the sales clerk a dollar, how much change are you going to get back?"

Nevertheless, they avoid complex activities and seldom expect students to discover for themselves how to solve difficult problems—complex challenges were not explored.

Teachers described their math lessons in fairly similar ways. They usually demonstrated step-by-step procedures for solving problems. They commonly used games to help children persist when learning complex concepts such as renaming in subtraction. These games were usually computational activities where teams, sometimes boys against girls, compete to complete a problem. One teacher described a relay race in which each team member completes part of a problem, to see which team can finish first. Sherita's description of a daily math lesson was typical. "I put the problems on the board and I tell them how I'm doing the problem. When we do word problems, I sort of make a game out of it."

Children completed a hefty quantity of assignments from workbooks, textbooks, and dittos, most of which involved computation and rote drill of facts. Although four of the teachers allowed students to work collaboratively, they worried that students copied from one another. The teachers also avoided any form of social comparison and minimized competition between individual students.

All but one teacher regularly used rewards in the classroom and made their children aware of how they could gain these rewards. Rewards included toys, school supplies, candy, and food. Most gave rewards to enhance motivation for lower achievers. Without rewards they could not get these children to learn.

"I have used small gifts, candy, stickers," Linda told me. "Sometimes I use the point system where they earn points for things. I use rewards for harder activities, something that may cause them stress or something very tedious. That's where I bring out reinforcers. They tend to increase their level of motivation. In third and fourth grades I use the reinforcements when we have times tables so they will get motivated to practice daily. I found it's better when I notice a lack of motivation and lack of effort to just pull out something new. Sometimes the classroom atmosphere is negative, so before someone acts out, I pull out something. I used more rewards when I taught at my other school because the children had less motivation and less parental support."

All of the teachers mentioned lack of parental support. They gave varied reasons for the lack of parental involvement, but most agreed that this is the result of a changing society. They see many parents who are concerned about their child's progress, but because of the demands of simply earning a living, these parents do not have the time to assist their children with schoolwork. Teachers thought that some parents lack the educational background to effectively help their children. The teachers said if parents don't get involved and encourage students, it is very unlikely the teacher will be successful in helping them learn. I asked if teaching could produce an ideally motivated student without strong parental support.

"Teaching can't really produce a highly motivated student," said Sherita, who was typical. "It helps, but it can't take the place of the parent. It [motivation] comes from home. It comes even before the child even enters school. When a child is first learning to walk and the parents say, 'Come on, you can do it, baby, come on and walk,' and the parents hold out their arms. That's motivation, that's what motivation means."

I found it disconcerting that teachers thought that most urban African-American children cannot cope with intellectual challenge. These teachers seemed to tell me that learning tasks should be comfortable and easily digested. They camouflage math lessons as games and use trinkets and bribes to coerce children into learning. These caring teachers seem to be captured by the children's living conditions and often chaotic home lives and try to shield them from difficult challenges and failure. Could this attempt to protect children inadvertently be teaching them not to think or function independently? In trying to help these children feel good about themselves, the teachers might be shielding them from the excitement of discovery.

THE SEARCH FOR BETTER MATH INSTRUCTION

After school started in the fall, three of my African-American teachers volunteered to work with me to see what could be learned from the interviews. I chose to invite these three because they were good teachers and we had become good friends over the years. I gave each a copy of the interview transcripts. I really needed their input. I needed to know if they were like the teachers I interviewed. I had supported some of the practices, like cooperative learning and not making comparisons of student ability. Nevertheless, I was bothered by the use of rewards, the predominance of computation and drill of facts, and the avoidance of complex activities. I wondered whether my teachers thought children can't cope with challenging problems. Did they use trinkets to bribe students into learning? Would they be ready to try something new?

The teachers filed into my office, smiling yet unsure. I asked them to tell me what they thought about the views that emerged and turned on my tape recorder. They readily accepted the value of avoiding public comparison of scores and of displaying grades. Next, we talked about the use of extrinsic rewards. I was surprised to find out that my teachers often use rewards to encourage the children. Although I am in classrooms nearly everyday, I never thought to check whether teachers use this practice. The teachers described rewards as essential for helping children learn. Ms. Potts, who used rewards extensively the previous year, was the only one who commented on the drawbacks.

"I can tell you from experience that too many 'prizes' are disastrous. My class last year got prizes for this and that, and I discovered that either they didn't care if they got the prize or they only tried to do the work to get the prize. And the skills weren't sticking."

"I give rewards, not often, only once in awhile," said Mrs. Harris, defending the practice.

"You don't feel there's any harm in that?" I ask.

"No, everyone expects to get something for good performance. Children don't understand 'learning for the sake of knowledge.' It's not until later that they recognize it."

Mrs. Harris's comment was disturbing. I had hoped that my teachers would not be like the ones I interviewed. I had hoped that they would see that our children can find learning intrinsically meaningful. Only now I recall that I had used rewards myself when I taught and once believed them necessary. I try not to show my disappointment, but I feel as if I'm being stabbed in the back by a loyal supporter. "Et tu, Brute!"

Mrs. Harris continues, "I don't believe that teachers who work with inner-city students are the only ones who use rewards."

"No, but almost all of the inner-city teachers I talked to said that they had to use rewards or incentives to motivate their students," I reply.

Mrs. Harris leans back in her chair, obviously thinking seriously. "I guess it's easier to say, 'If you learn your multiplication tables I have a gift for you.' We do need to excite these children in other ways," she admits.

After some discussion, we agree that if teachers were unable to use rewards they might come up with more interesting lessons to excite the children about learning. Rewards offer an easy way for teachers to convince themselves that students are learning.

"Kids really like personal experiences. That's a really good motivation," Ms. Potts adds and we latch on to the topic of "playing grocery store." This practice is common in our school and does not offer a new way to help children learn better, so I prod them to move on.

In the interviews, six teachers said that they concentrate on computational skills and none said that they allowed students to choose problems or activities. Now we consider possible reasons for this emphasis. My teachers agree that part of the problem is that teachers are expected to prepare students for standardized tests and, therefore, concentrate on the skills their students need to get through those tests. They also blame administrators and parents who hold teachers responsible if the students are not on a certain page in the book by the end of the grading period.

Mrs. Harris raises another point. "Most math books are set up so that the concept is introduced and then steps are taught to solve the problem. The teachers, for the most part, briefly go over the concept but drill on the computational steps."

"We do have a problem with that," Ms. Potts agrees.

"I'm guilty of that," Mrs. Harris confesses. "My students will come to me and say 'I don't know what to do.' Instead of encouraging them to sit down and think it out, I'll go over the steps. But children, if given the time and the opportunity, can think through math problems. But that's the problem. It might take them forever and we don't have that kind of time. We are still responsible for a certain amount of work to be completed to get them through the tests. The slower students would take a lot longer."

Mrs. Harris's concern about preparing students for standardized tests reminds me of a comment by Holt (1964). They seem to agree with his point that

> A week or two before the [standardized] tests, their teachers begin an intensive drilling on all the kinds of problems they will have to do on the test. By the time the test comes along the children are conditioned, like Pavlov's dog; when they see a certain arrangement of numerals and symbols before them, lights begin to flash, wheels begin to turn, and like robots they go through the answer-getting process, or enough of them to get a halfway decent score. Teachers are not supposed to do this; but they all do. So did I. (p. 154)

My teachers go on to agree that it would be beneficial to allow children to become more involved by providing opportunities for them to think through solutions to problems and to have them make more decisions and choices in classroom activities. They also agree that they should give more opportunities to explore complex, challenging math activities. This would increase students' involvement, allowing them to become active learners. Teachers, they say, should help students to think for themselves. But, they inform me, there is a problem. The obstacle of time limitations would have to be removed. "The administrator," they say, "could not demand that teachers cover a certain amount of work in a certain amount of time." "Teachers," they go on, "must be more independent and use their best professional judgment to adapt lessons to the needs of their students."

I begin to feel that this conversation is more hypothetical than real to my teachers. They referred to "the administrator" and "teachers," not "you" and "me." I decide to go out on a limb by asking if they will support what they are saying and try to teach math using what they have suggested.

Mrs. Hill answers first. "I'll be going out on maternity leave in a few months so it would just be too confusing for my students."

"I have too much work to cover with my class," Ms. Potts explains. "They're really behind in math. I don't think this is a good idea for them."

"I'll give it a try," says Mrs. Harris, who seems surprised these words came out of her mouth. What a relief—one teacher is willing to try.

Over the next couple of weeks, Mrs. Harris and I met several times to decide how to begin with her fourth-grade class. We tried to find ways to teach so the children would be free to think more independently. Our primary goal was to involve the students in more complex, challenging math problems and encourage them to explore different ways of solving these problems. This, we hoped, would allow the students to become more involved in their task and more motivated to do mathematics.

We decided textbooks would be eliminated, at least in the beginning stages, until Mrs. Harris felt that it was appropriate to reintroduce them. We felt the textbooks could easily become a crutch. They are full of procedural steps of solving problems and do not allow enough opportunities for students to explore possibilities.

As we discussed ways to challenge students' thinking, lots of ideas came up. Perhaps students might keep logs of their own work or work in small groups and collaborate to solve problems. We decided to start by having Mrs. Harris talk with her class about these ideas before the math lessons were changed. In the classroom we tape-recorded her conversation with the students so that we could discuss it later.

MATHEMATICS THROUGH STUDENTS' EYES

"Before we start our next lesson," says Mrs. Harris, "I want to ask you a few questions. Be real honest. I want you to say how you feel."

The children look anxious and begin wiggling in their seats.

"Don't look so worried. The questions are about math."

This is apparently not the topic the students anticipated, and Mrs. Harris is momentarily interrupted by a chorus of moans.

"Yes, math. My first question is, how do you feel about math?"

Lakita, an honor student who usually gets As in math, is the first to respond. She is the classroom social star, outspoken and sometimes domineering. She is also one of the smartest math students in the class.

"I think it's stupid!" The children laugh.

"I think it's fun because when you go to the store you know how much to pay," answers Sandra.

"I like it," says Tim.

"I think it's dumb, hard, and boring," Johnny insists.

"I like math because it helps me count and I like times tables," Valencia remarks.

Mrs. Harris continues her poll of the class, seeking out the children who have so far been reluctant to speak.

Tammy, looking very serious and thoughtful, says, "I think it's important, but boring because we have to spend so much time listening to you."

From the back of the room Michael shouts, "It makes me sick!" The students, enjoying Michael's candor, begin laughing and look at me to see if I am going to tell them to stop.

Kaye adds, "Boring, and it wastes too much time." Mrs. Harris looks surprised that many of her students feel this way about math. She felt it was her best subject. I am also surprised, because I believed she was as competent as any of my teachers at math.

The noise in the room increases as the children share and clarify their feelings.

Mrs. Harris asks if there is anything about math that is fun. One child responds that he likes math games. Another says she enjoys working with money. The rest stray away from the question and comment on how they feel math might be useful in the future when they are grown up. Mrs. Harris steers the students back to what in particular they think is fun to do in math.

"Pretending you're a rich man and adding up more and more money!" says Michael, again amusing his classmates.

The children tell the kinds of computation they enjoy, addition, rounding off, and so on.

Mrs. Harris asks, "Who feels that math is not a lot of fun." The hands quickly go up. Larry, a low achiever in math who rarely speaks in class, is first.

"It's hard."

"You waste a lot of paper and it's real hard," adds Johneva.

Lakita again gives her opinion, "I don't like it because you have to think."

I find her remark puzzling because she is a high achiever in math. Lakita's comment brings more giggles and other unfavorable comments. A student shouts that she doesn't like math because they can't use calculators.

"I don't like it because when you're working on a long hard problem you start sweating," Larry adds.

Mrs. Harris probes for several minutes asking the students about the content and practices of her math lessons. She then asks the children what parts of math they don't like. Larry is first again.

"I don't like solving the problems."

"I don't like to think very hard," says Michael. Again the class finds him very amusing.

"I don't like subtraction where you have to rename," Kaye adds. Others agree.

Mrs. Harris slightly changes the subject by asking the children why they believed they have to learn math. As I later found out, Mrs. Harris had discussed this question with the children many times. The students answer as she had taught them. "When you get grown and stuff you have to count your money," says David. Every child who speaks gives a similar answer: Math is needed "when you get grown" to pay the bills, to go to the store, and to keep from getting cheated.

The children, obviously enjoying their conversation, begin talking louder among themselves. Larry makes a comment and Mrs. Harris asks him to share it with the rest of the class. As he speaks, I listen carefully because Larry rarely volunteers to answer a question or give a comment. He is usually invisible during math class.

"The only thing fun about math is when you finish your work."

"Do you mean when you finish your math you feel good about it?" Softly Larry replies, "No."

"Do you mean the only thing you like about math is to be finished with your math problems because you don't want to do math just be finished with it?"

"Yes," he says.

Mrs. Harris asks the children to comment on the way that math is taught in her classroom.

Lakita, the first to say math is stupid, knows well how to manipulate teachers and is again first, "I think you teach math great and you're a good math teacher." She looks confident that she has said the right thing. All of the children support Lakita and say that they like the way Mrs. Harris teaches math. All except Michael. Even though he makes the children laugh again, he seems quite sincere, not merely trying to create a laugh, when he tells Mrs. Harris her classes are dull. The children's remarks are confusing. They seem to agree that they like their teacher but find little value or enjoyment in her math lessons.

As we had planned, Mrs. Harris then asks if the children would like to learn math a different way. She explains that they might work to discover ways to solve math problems without using their textbook all the time. They would be allowed to decide what math problems they would work on. They also would work together in groups and discuss the best way to solve the problems. Maybe they could even decide how many different ways a particular problem could be solved. They could have plenty of time to think about the problem, and they would not get a bad grade if they did not come up with the right answer right away. Instead they would think about each problem and discuss the best way to solve it. (These ideas came in part from Cobb, Yackel, & Wood, 1988.) We both expected the children to be excited about this proposal.

"I'd feel I was cheated every time I bought something at the store," Ryan answers.

"I wouldn't like it," says Johnny.

The rest of the class agrees. I am surprised and Mrs. Harris looks stunned that the children are not willing to change their math lessons even though they now don't enjoy them. Her glance at me says "Help! Where do we go now?" She tries to reassure them.

"We're going to work on math problems, but there wouldn't be a right way or a wrong way to do them."

The students are not comforted.

"I wouldn't like it because I would probably get a bad grade," Johnny remarks in a worried tone.

"This won't be for grades," Mrs. Harris counters. "This is about discovering for yourself."

The children remain uneasy. A girl in the back of the room fears that she will get all of her problems wrong.

"I wouldn't like it because you would say, 'That's wrong, try it over again!'"

"What makes math more interesting to you?" Mrs. Harris asks.

"When we don't have a lot of problems to do!" Johnny quickly responds.

Again the children began talking among themselves and Mrs. Harris reminds the class that each must share his or her ideas with the entire class.

"I liked math in kindergarten," someone shouts.

"In second grade the teacher told stories to go along with the pictures in the math book," another child says.

"Why do we have word problems?" someone asks.

"How could I make math more fun for you?" Mrs. Harris asks her students.

"Have cartoon characters," says Michael.

"Shop with catalogs and play money," Ryan adds.

The children eagerly shout out suggestions.

"More games."

"Do only four problems."

"Draw pictures on the board."

"Video games."

"Less problems."

The students' apprehension reminds me of two articles written by Lisa Delpit (1986, 1988). She complains that, among others, African-American teachers have been left out of any dialogue on how best to educate African-American students. Many of them see direct instruction, focusing on basic skills and information, as the best way to educate these children. She argues that when exposed to romantic progressive education techniques, African-American students often feel that the teachers are cheating them out of their education. Delpit (1988) described an African-American doctoral student who was assigned to a process-method writing class. Students in this class worked in groups to edit one anothers' papers. The student described his anger and disappointment in the teacher.

> I didn't feel she was teaching us anything. She wanted us to correct each others' papers and we were there to learn from her. She didn't teach anything, absolutely nothing. (p. 287)

Delpit (1988) continues, "The students . . . seem to be saying that the teacher has denied them access to herself as the source of knowledge necessary to learn the forms they need to succeed" (p. 288). Sosniak and Perlman (1990) find that African-American and Hispanic high school students "seem to experience considerable frustration with mathematics when teachers ask them to do work on their own, without extended teacher demonstration and explanation" (p. 430). Our students seem to have the same concern. Without Mrs. Harris's direct instruction, the students believe they can't learn anything. The point of math for them is to learn to deal with financial calculations, to follow the teacher's directives, and give the correct answer. They don't like the system, but don't want to change for fear they will lose out. Perhaps after we start our project, their fears will evaporate.

NEW DIRECTIONS

Mrs. Harris and I meet the next day. We decide the math lessons should be changed gradually. Perhaps the first step would be allowing the students more time to think through solutions and encouraging them in this process instead of teaching the steps in solving the problems.

In a few weeks I return to Mrs. Harris's classroom. The children are discussing multiplying two, two-digit numbers. As I enter, they stop talking and look at me. Mrs. Harris brings them back.

"Bobby just put a problem on the board [36 × 45]. He would like to solve this problem, but he doesn't need to know the exact answer, he needs an estimation. Remember we talked about estimating. Now think about what you want to multiply."

No one responds. Mrs. Harris is used to relying on Lakita and calls her to the board. "Lakita can you think of a way of solving this problem?"

Mrs. Harris tells the class that if they disagree with Lakita they should raise their hands so that they can help. Although eager to respond, Lakita seems to have no idea what has been asked of her. Mrs. Harris then calls on Anthony who says, "It would be easier to estimate the problem first. Change the 36 to 40 and change the 45 to 50. Then you multiply the 40 × 50."

Anthony goes to the board and writes down 200 as the answer. No one comments on his error and the room falls quiet. Mrs. Harris invites the students to think about this answer. Some students say the answer is correct, but most remain silent. Rather than point out the inaccuracy, Mrs. Harris asks the children to think of a way to check the answer. Kaye quickly answers that addition can be used. April then says to add 40 to 40 fifty times. A few agree that this will produce the correct answer. Mrs. Harris encourages them each to try to solve the problem using addition.

"I have an answer of 2,100," Ryan says. He also noted that it was easier to add up 50 forty times because he could count by five and "go faster." Ryan seems to have realized that he can discover ways to use numbers. This is what we hoped for. At Mrs. Harris's request, Ryan comes to the board to show the rest of the class his method. He walks up to Mrs. Harris and shows her his paper. She again asks him to show it on the board. As he writes down the 50s and counts by five he corrects his error and gives an answer of 2,000. Tammy agrees that 2,000 is correct.

Mrs. Harris says, "Class, let's go back to my original question. Does 40×50 equal 200?" The children then agree that Anthony's original answer is incorrect.

Lakita, who was eager to answer but had no idea how, objects, "We haven't discussed these kinds of problems in math."

"That's true," Mrs. Harris replies, "but you came up with the answer, didn't you?"

Not satisfied, Lakita approaches me. "Mrs. Harris shows us how to do it step by step and it's hard in a way to do it the new way."

The children discuss other problems of multiplying tens by tens. They are slow in inventing ideas and the atmosphere is sluggish.

As the session ends, Fred brings me his paper to show me that he had multiplied 36×45, and his answer is correct. Fred is competent doing computation and usually gets good grades.

Mrs. Harris announces the end of the session and collects the papers. Larry, who used to hate math and performed poorly, is still engrossed in a problem.

Later that afternoon, Mrs. Harris and I talk about some of the children's resistance to the new approach. Mrs. Harris confided, "Lakita likes me to teach so that she has a guideline. She's a good thinker, but she's afraid. She'll ask me something several times to be sure before she puts anything on the paper. She does not want to be wrong. Michael didn't write anything down. He is a good thinker, but . . ."

We discuss Fred, who could multiply 46×35 and wanted me to know that. Like most of the others, he could not see that 40×50 could not be 200. "He was only taught how to do it," says Mrs. Harris. "He never had to figure out how to do it or what it means. It's hard to break away from habits."

Except for Larry, most had written very little. Mrs. Harris commented on Larry's new involvement in class. "He called me over. He was still concerned about understanding the problem even after I had collected the other children's papers. He's not as frightened of math as he used to be."

We still have a problem of getting all the children really involved. As I observe the children working it appears that half of the students are not doing math. They talk and play. Some take a rest period or draw doodles on their papers. Mrs. Harris, however, is gaining enthusiasm as she sees Theresa, Larry, Ryan, and a few others rise to the occasion and find innovative ways to solve the problems. She emphasizes high points.

"Theresa is slow, especially in math. I am very surprised when she raises her hand. I don't ever remember her doing that. I have also noticed that the children helped each other more. At the beginning they were reluctant and would cover their papers so that no one would see their answers. They don't do that anymore. They are more likely to work together, now it's become part of the classroom procedure, but it had to be encouraged. It was even difficult to get them to talk to each other in a group. They would sit together, sit next to each other, and not help each other. When I'd ask how come they weren't helping each other, I would hear, 'Well he didn't do it right! I did it like this!'"

As the weeks progressed I periodically sat in on the math classes. As Christmas vacation approached, I could see that math lessons had really changed. The children now work together in pairs or small groups, choosing the topics to work on from options given by Mrs. Harris. Mrs. Harris uses the challenge and enrichment activities from Harper Row Mathematics (1985), which require students to figure out solutions. In some activities, students are given the answers to problems and look for different ways to come to a solution.

One activity involves division patterns, where digits are missing in the dividend or quotient. Students have to look for multiples of the divisor or add the remainder to find the missing digits. Some of the multistep problems continue for several days. For example, students make number puzzles designed like crossword puzzles, where across and down division problems are used instead of word clues. Here students have to write division problems, solve them, and arrange them so that they fit into a mathematical puzzle. Sharing is essential, with each group discussing problem solutions and techniques. Difficulties and failed attempts at problem solving are shared as well. They keep their logs and occasionally use the math text as a reference when sample problems are needed or for clues to procedural steps. When a concept is difficult, students rewrite the problem and the solution from the text in their own mathematical language and use the information later. Students designed a way of showing the relationship between fractions, decimals, and measurement in centimeters by rewriting the textbook explanation to something similar to a French-English dictionary.

Some of the projects continue as homework with parents and grandparents helping. I was especially happy that the projects were beginning to involve parents. On one of my visits the class discussed a homework assignment.

"I came home real mad that I had this hard problem. I had a lot of people helping me. Then I called my mother at work and she helped me," said Tammy.

Sandra adds, "At first we thought it was real hard, but then we thought about it . . ."

Before Sandra finishes, Ryan's excitement overtakes him and he interrupts with, "My grandmother wanted to see it to see if she could tackle it. I told her my whole class couldn't figure it out. Then my mom came home from work. She corrected my grandmother and that's how I came out with the answer."

In the past, getting homework assignments completed had been difficult, especially with students who needed help. Rather than get their parents involved, some children would tell their parents that they had no assignment. The enthusiasm with which these children talked suggested that we, the school, had approached the issue of homework incorrectly. Perhaps it is the nature of the assignment that led students to resist rather than the very idea of homework. If tasks could be made interesting and challenging enough to require collaborative effort, perhaps students and their parents would delight in problem solving.

Some of the children are not yet fully involved. We are concerned and discuss what the problem might be and whether we should continue. Mrs. Harris gives me some insight.

"We [teachers] have done this. It's easier to teach a lesson by giving the students an example and showing them how to compute, than to allow the students the time to think through a problem. It's part of our classroom control. This class may not get used to thinking through math problems and getting involved in their own learning until the end of the school year or even next year."

We make some decisions about the next lessons and part for the afternoon. Mrs. Harris's optimistic realism is encouraging.

The new lessons continue and periodically I stop in to see how the class is doing. Most children seem busy, yet some are no more motivated than they were before.

Both Mrs. Harris and Lisa Delpit mention control in the classroom. Delpit (1988) suggests that many African-American teachers "control" their students by exhibiting "personal power." Black students, she suggests see a good teacher as one who is authoritarian, who gives directives and "pushes" the students. She says these authoritarian teachers give their students explicit directives and are not afraid to express power in the classroom. She explains that black children operate under a notion of authority different from that of white middle-class children and may feel that middle-class teachers who use progressive education techniques may be perceived as weak and ineffective. Delpit (1988) writes,

Black children expect an authority figure to act with authority. When the teacher instead acts as a "chum," the message sent is that this adult has no authority, and the children react accordingly. . . . Many people of color expect authority to be earned by personal efforts and exhibited by personal characteristics. In other words, "the authoritative person gets to be a teacher because she is authoritative." (p. 289)

I have some difficulty with these ideas, but I am afraid she might be right. I decide I must, in the future, ask Mrs. Harris to read the Delpit article and discuss it with me.

It is now February. Mrs. Harris and I have decided that we will discuss with the students how they feel about the activities so far. We had expected that by this time the students would be more excited and more involved in their learning. Perhaps we are missing something, and if this is true perhaps the students can help us. I talk with some of the students, and they tell me they don't like to figure out the problems.

I ask, "If you can figure out the problems, why don't you like to work out the steps by yourself? Eventually you can figure out the answer, right?"

"Yes," the students answer.

"While you're figuring out the problems, what are you doing?"

A few understand.

"Thinking," they answer.

I ask if they prefer the old way Mrs. Harris taught them or the "new" way of exploring possibilities of solving problems.

Mark answered, "I like the old way Mrs. Harris taught us. The other way we might not understand it."

"But do you understand what you are doing?"

"Yes."

I then ask, if they understand after they figure it out, why don't they like to solve the math problems without their teacher telling them the steps to do first?

Mark quickly answers, "You have to think about it and thinking is boring!"

I turned to Larry, who has often seemed interested and has worked hard.

"Larry, how did you feel about the lessons?"

Larry answers, "They're hard."

I begin to feel that I had not convinced anyone to explore math. Perhaps this is the wrong course. But Fred keeps me going.

"I like it," he says.

Mrs. Harris and I decide to continue with the lessons even though many say that they prefer learning the "old" way.

THE SEARCH CONTINUES

Weeks later, Mrs. Harris asks me to visit her classroom. The children are covering mathematical patterns finding the square of a number [7 × 7 = 49] and comparing the product when one factor is 1 more and the other factor is 1 less than the number [8 × 6 = 48]. She has asked me to bring my oversized calculator so the children can use it. There is a large group of children working in the middle of the room. When I give them the calculator, they become very excited. They take turns punching in the numbers. They are all very eager and are squirming out of their seats. This is the most excitement I have seen from many of them since we started this project.

They begin by having a student give the square of 70. Several students take turns punching in the numbers and writing down the answer. Then 1 less than 70 and 1 more than 70. One student punches in the 69, another the multiplication symbol, another the 71, and finally the equal sign. They copy down the product. A student who has had a turn using the calculator reaches for it again and is immediately stopped by shouts of "You had a turn!"

The children are discussing the patterns. 70 × 70 = 4,900 and 69 × 71 is 1 less or 4,899. They move on to patterns of 2 more and 2 less. Mrs. Harris and I move around the classroom and listen. Some students work in pairs discussing the patterns. Still, some have to be coaxed into getting started. Frederic is ready and eager to give the answer to his group. I ask him to wait and give the others a chance to think it out.

As I continue to move around to observe progress, I notice Larry staring straight ahead, barely blinking. I decide not to disturb him. He is either thinking or has totally blanked out. I reassure myself that he must be thinking. I see some children writing down all kinds of numbers. Some of the numbers do not seem remotely connected to the problem. As I step back and watch, I can see that they understand how to find the pattern.

Mrs. Harris asks Candy to explain what pattern her group has come up with. Candy, a very quiet and tiny little girl who often does not speak much louder than a whisper, says she will try. She, like Larry, had been afraid of math and afraid to try. Looking confident, Candy explains how she worked through the patterns. I feel very good about her new confidence and pleasure with math. I sense that Mrs. Harris feels the same because she smiles and nods her head.

Some of the children are up to patterns of 4 more and 4 less. As I walk around the room again, Marie, Theresa, and Candy are beaming together. Still, some have not fully participated. They do not volunteer any suggestions and rely on the others in their group to do the work. Mrs. Harris moves around to coax them into getting involved.

Several weeks later Mrs. Harris has invited me to visit her classroom again. She wants me to talk to them about the project. Some still resist thinking and participating in discussions, even when they seem to know how to do the problems.

"Are you thinking through problems in math?" I ask the class.

In unison, the children respond "yes." I then ask them what they think about these problems. One student answers that she thinks they are hard.

Larry, who had once said the new way was hard, volunteers, "It's kind of easy."

"Do you enjoy doing the work?" I ask.

"I think it's fun," says Candy, who hardly ever spoke in class under the old system, "because you have more time to think about it. Mrs. Harris gives us a lot of time, but sometimes if you don't understand the old way you might go real slow, and you won't be through and you still don't understand. When you get through thinking about it this new way, you can understand a little better."

Lakita is still complaining. "This is harder because you have to think more."

"How many feel the problems are hard?"

All but a few hands go up.

"How many think the problems are fun?"

Most of the same hands go up. I'm surprised that so many of the slower math students raise their hands.

Candy explains, "It's hard, but it's fun when you do it and have to think about it."

Many agree with Candy. Some don't say anything.

"How do you feel when you're thinking out these problems? Do you feel smarter?"

Tamarra answers first. "I do. I feel smarter and I usually do bad in math."

April agrees that she, too, feels smarter.

I then ask the children how many feel smarter. About half the class— Anthony, Theresa, Lori, Larry, April, Kaye, Candy, Michael, Fred, and Tamarra—raise their hands.

Lakita is still protesting. "I'm used to a teacher explaining step by step. When we do math this new way, I can figure it out but it takes more time."

"Is that good or bad?" I ask.

"Bad."

"Don't you want to continue the math this new way?"

Lakita, Tammy, Kaye, and Johnny answer no. Lakita angrily motions to the students who are sitting next to her to join her in protest. I can hear her say to them in a low but determined voice, "Say no! Say no!"

"How many are enjoying the math lessons?"

Most of the students raise their hands, including those who said they felt smarter. With a little encouragement, I convince the class to continue the lessons.

At the end of the session I was glad that I had put the question to the children as to whether we should continue or not. One concern is that the children we formerly considered the brightest, especially Lakita and Kaye, had not wanted to continue. They become angry and frustrated when Mrs. Harris does not tell them directly how to solve a problem. When Cobb, Yackel, and Wood (1988) tried to introduce their problem-centered approach to math, they found

> that the children's beliefs about the teacher's role changed with the realization that they were obliged to resolve their problems for themselves and that they were not obliged to use any particular solution. Their beliefs about the nature of mathematical activity also changed once they accepted and attempted to fulfill this obligation. (p. 142)

It may take a while before Lakita and a few others come to a new understanding of Mrs. Harris's role and their own intellectual autonomy.

Right now, the positive outweighs the negative. Those who had been slower math students are much more involved. Larry and a few others are steadily more active. Parents have become more involved because students discuss and share their math projects at home. Many have said that they feel smarter. Undoubtedly, they are more confident now that they can figure out much of their math work. A promising sign is that the word *fun* was used. It had taken a whole math period to solve one problem and many said it was fun. April had said the fun was the "challenge." Most seemed to agree by the time I left the session that "hard" was not a bad thing, hard meant thinking more, and thinking was good.

The school year is rapidly coming to an end. I take time from a busy day to visit the fourth-grade class. As I enter the room a few children look up but most do not notice me. They are consumed with the day's assignment. Mrs. Harris is working with a group. As I approach this group, Lakita quickly explains why her group is being taught the "old way."

"We didn't understand," she tells me, meaning they needed help.

Mrs. Harris gives me a quick smile and continues. I decide not to disturb them. I move around the room to observe the other children.

Some look up briefly to show me what they are doing and then continue. Most are too engrossed to notice me. I notice that Michael, who once said Mrs. Harris's math classes were boring, is absorbed in his work. I decide to return to my office. I'm not needed here anymore. The children have changed. Hard math now means an interesting challenge. Self-esteem is not a concern here. Hard work does not "tear them down." It builds them up. Parents are concerned and want to be involved when students are excited about what they are accomplishing in school. Parents are interested in what their children find interesting in school. When students are excited about assignments given for homework, parents are more likely to support and help with homework assignments. The parents of these students have proved this is true.

It still troubles me that Lakita and some of the others still prefer the "old way." Mrs. Harris, however, has no doubts that she is on a better course. Perhaps she is correct that it may take more than one school year for students to adapt. It may not have been fair to them. They have been dependent on us. This is the way that we have taught them to be. We changed the rules in the middle of the game. Lakita's grades had been As under the old system. She followed the teachers' directions, paid attention, was quiet, and did not question. She did the right thing. Her good grades told her this. She was never asked to investigate or explore possibilities. The teacher was always in control of what they learned and how much. She set the pace and drew the limits. Active learning was never demanded. I understand Lakita's confusion and frustration. Even Mrs. Hill and Ms. Potts had fears that perhaps this project was not a good idea for their students. That idea occurred to me, especially when some students continued to resist. I wanted math to be meaningful to them, but there was some apprehension that giving them freedom to explore might lead them nowhere. Now I am glad that I took a chance and broke with the routine and invited Mrs. Harris to invite her students to take a similar risk. The project has been good for the students and for me. It has made me more aware of what is really going on in the classrooms. I knew which students make the honor roll and which students get failing grades. I thought I knew everything important that went on in my school. It was all routine. I did not notice many things, like the bells that ring every day at the same time. It was not only the bells that I did not hear. My demands to complete the curriculum contributed to the problem. Mrs. Harris had talked to me several times about control. I realize now what she meant—teachers "control" students with no real connection to them as thinkers. By controlling the curriculum, principals control teachers, too, without provoking real thought.

Later that afternoon, Mrs. Harris came to my office to return the Delpit (1986, 1988) articles I had asked her to read. I turn on the recorder.

"Now I agree that many of the points Delpit brings up do exist and are reality," she tells me. "But if we continue to teach by giving directives and being authoritarian, our children will continue to feel as if they are being policed and should be policed. We do tell black students what to do. We want control, but only because that is what we and they are used to. Parents do this, even before the children start school. This is because the parents were 'told' what to do and their parents were 'told' what to do. It was part of the slave culture and they had to do it. Those were directives. Slaves gave directives to their children. When they came in from the field, they told their children to eat and turn out the light and go to bed. But let's go back to the 'slaves' that did not take directives, those who were not obedient. Those were the inventors and scientists. The ones that did not follow directives. Instead of turning out the light, they lit a candle and read. I'm sure no one said to [George Washington] Carver, 'Take this peanut and invent something.' Instead he was thinking, 'What if . . .' Those inventors and scientists took the initiative to think through something. Our parents had the same idea about giving children 'directives' that Delpit mentions. It is part of our culture. But as you learn or learn differently you do things differently. Just because she says certain things are part of our culture and they exist in the classroom does not mean they should remain. She mentioned black teachers. Well, as black teachers we have learned that there are other ways to reach our students. Let them think for themselves. You'd be surprised what they come up with."

My old concerns now have been replaced by new ones. I am not sure how to deal with the "Lakitas." These "good" students may make it hard for teachers to teach well. We have to give such students new reasons for doing math. We have a faculty meeting planned for next week. Mrs. Harris and I are going to talk to the other teachers about the project and how we hope to continue next year. Over the past months Mrs. Harris has discussed her students with some of the teachers, most of whom are doubtful but curious. On one issue I totally agree with Lisa Delpit (1988): that is, her concern that minority teachers have been left out of the dialogue on the best ways to educate minority children. She has also stated that parents and members of poor communities "must be allowed to participate fully in the discussion of what kind of instruction is in their children's best interest" (p. 296). We need also to include our students in this dialogue. It was important that I should understand how my students felt about their math classes, even when they did not tell me what

I expected to hear. I am impressed by Mrs. Harris's insights, and I am eager to see if my other teachers are equally impressed.

I am making a few notes about my last classroom visit when I hear the dismissal bell. I stop for a few minutes and go outside to say goodbye to the children.

REFERENCES

Cobb, P., Yackel, E., & Wood, T. (1988). Young children's emotional acts while doing mathematical problem solving. In D. B. Mcleod & V. M. Adams (Eds.), *Affect and problem solving: A new perspective* (pp. 117–148). New York: Springer-Verlag.

Delpit, L. D. (1986). Skills and other dilemmas of a progressive black educator. *Harvard Educational Review, 56,* 379–385.

Delpit, L. D. (1988). The silenced dialogue: Power and pedagogy in educating other people's children. *Harvard Educational Review, 58,* 280–298.

Holt, J. (1964). *How children fail.* New York: Dell.

Sosniak, L. A., & Perlman, C. L. (1990). Secondary education by the book. *Journal of Curriculum Studies, 22,* 427–442.

6 Students as Collaborators in Curriculum Construction

SCIENCE AND TOLERANCE

John G. Nicholls, University of Illinois at Chicago
Susan P. Hazzard, Happy Hollow School

Susan Hazzard and students

John Dewey argued that students should be involved in the formation of the purposes that govern their activities. They should, in negotiation with their fellows, shape their own motives or reasons for learning—they should be involved in forming their curriculum and in reflecting on its value. Yet there was little of this in Dewey's school or anywhere since. This chapter is a report of an attempt, in a second-grade classroom, to breathe life into Dewey's vision.

"There is, I think," wrote John Dewey (1938), "no point in the philosophy of progressive education which is sounder than its emphasis upon the importance of the participation of the learner in the formation of the purposes which direct his [or her] activities in the learning process" (p. 67). Despite Dewey's influence, students are rarely provoked to ask what knowledge or what purposes they should pursue in school (Erickson & Shultz, 1992). Progressive education, like democracy, is one of those ideas that has barely been tried (but see Boomer, Lester, Onore, & Cook, 1992).

Mayhew and Edwards (1936) describe Dewey's laboratory school at the University of Chicago as seeking to regain a time

> when there was no rift between experience and [school] knowledge, when information about things and ways of doing grew out of social situations and represented answers to social needs, when the education of the immature member of society proceeded almost wholly through participation in the social or community life of which he was a member, and each individual, no matter how young, did certain things in the way of work and play *along* with others, and learned, thereby, to adjust himself to his surroundings, to adapt himself to social relationships, and to get control of his own special powers. (p. 21)

Their concern for meaningful learning and connected social and intellectual life is apparent. Yet Mayhew and Edwards do not picture students as involved in negotiating the curriculum in the manner that Dewey appeared to suggest they should.

One eight-year-old in Dewey's school asked his teacher, "Which do you think . . . is the best way to study geography—to begin with your own place and go out, out, out, until you reach the stars, or to begin with the stars and come in and in until you reach your own place again?" (Mayhew & Edwards, 1936, p. 289). He was told that people differ on this matter, but that this year the class would study his locality. He agreed, but murmured, "But I shall get a book about the stars, anyway" (Mayhew & Edwards, 1936, p. 289).

This boy might have been taken more seriously, for two reasons. First, the assumption that what is closest to the child's home will be closest to his or her heart as a topic for study is, as this boy hinted, questionable. Involvement might be heightened more by the unknown than by the commonplace. Second, his reasons for wanting to start his studies

---

This chapter is based on sections of J. G. Nicholls and S. P. Hazzard (1993). *Education as adventure: Lessons from the second grade*. New York: Teachers College Press.

far from home remained unexamined. He and his classmates might have been challenged to reflect on why knowledge of the stars is of value.

The disposition to ask intelligently, "Why learn this stuff?" is central to Dewey's vision of democratic education. For him, freedom meant "the power to frame purposes and to execute purposes so framed. . . . Plato once defined a slave as the person who executes the purposes of another, and . . . a person is also a slave who is enslaved to [her or] his own blind desires" (Dewey, 1938, p. 67). Thus the importance of educating desires by securing "the active co-operation of the pupil in the formation of the purposes involved in [her or] his studying" (Dewey, 1938, p. 67). In today's alternative schools, freedom to choose topics of study is common, but it is uncommon to find active negotiation of what knowledge is worth gaining (Korn, 1991). To choose without reflection on one's reasons for learning is not to intelligently form one's purposes. If students merely choose, they act as consumers rather than educational philosophers or curriculum theorists.

After a certain amount of collaborative blundering (Nicholls & Hazzard, 1993), we tried treating Sue Hazzard's second-grade students as educational theorists and collaborators in curriculum construction. We began with science education. The typical science class requires every student to "complete the same readings, worksheets, experiments and tests—and to come to essentially the same conclusions" (Goodlad, 1983, p. 215). Would students provoked to ask the questions, What is science? And what science should they "do"? break free of this dullness? Would the negotiation of the details and direction of the emerging curriculum produce a high intellectual adventure?

Sue's students trusted one another and were accustomed to the lively negotiation of other aspects of classroom life. Late in February, Sue began asking her students what science was, provoking them to justify their answers, helping them act on their ideas, and, again, provoking them to evaluate the curriculum they had created. They were not merely asked to choose or provoked to learn actively. They were provoked to reflect on the nature of scientific knowledge, on how one judges the adequacy of knowledge, and on what type of knowledge is most worthwhile. They were challenged to name, examine, and reconstruct their purposes in studying.

WHAT IS SCIENCE AND WHAT SCIENCE IS WORTHWHILE?

"What's the best way to learn about science?" asks Sue.

"Have a scientist instructor," is the rapid answer.

"Science projects."

"I like to see pictures," declares Dan. "Not just people telling. And it is neat how people can share ideas. Like, some of my friends have weird ideas. Ulp! I don't mean they're stupid. I think they are silly, but then I think about it, and it makes sense." Dan does not have to be taught the value of dialogue for fostering insight.

"Read books."

"Have a scientist here."

"Have a movie . . ."

"We could have an hour or 30 minutes and *do* things about science. Then we can write about it and tell it," says Peter, developing Dan's ideas.

"I think we should have experiments in the room," says Dan.

"How would you do it?" asks Sue.

"Use measuring things."

"Take time bombs and see what would happen," says James.

"How would you do experiments?" Sue repeats. "Would you want me to do them?"

"I want us to do it. Like on our desks," says Dan. "We could have a center and probably make a book about it."

"We could get paper and everyone can make a picture of what happens."

"We could send notes home asking for help to get materials," says Evelyn.

"I'd like to do them safely," urges Tim, thinking of time bombs.

Other possibilities are discussed. Then:

"What is science?" asks Sue.

"Learning."

"What happened in the past," says Claire, puzzling us for the moment.

"It's what happened in the film [we saw]."

"Wires."

"Engines."

"Water."

"Space."

"History."

"Can you explain more how history and science are like each other, Claire?" asks Sue.

"Like about the dinosaurs."

"Oh, yes!"

"Science is what you're thinking about and what you discover," says Peter, recognizing at some level that science is a human construction. His line of thought resonates.

"You go on trips and try to see what happens . . . you put a straw in water and . . ." says Alan.

"One thing I like in science is things from the past," says Paul.

"Maybe we can put all the information in the computer," suggests Alan.

"How will you know," asks Sue, "if the information is accurate?"

"Get different books and read them and get models and compare."

"Why would you want to go to more than one thing?"

"Computers don't know everything."

"To see if everyone thinks the same thing and if they do, it's probably true," suggests Vera.

"So you could read lots of things by many people we'd know? Peter, what do you think?"

He has been waving his hand to say, "Sometimes we like to be surprised. We like it if you do like with the pop rocks." He refers to an occasion when Sue presented an unexpected experience.

Dan reveals his enthusiasm for the emerging possibilities. "We don't always have fun at recess. They might stay in and do it. I mean stay in and do science, not math and stuff."

"I have a book on air-cushion vehicles and . . ."

"Should I teach science like reading?" asks Sue, to provoke further clarification. A chorus of no's indicates the inappropriateness of the idea. As they reveal in other ways, they approve of reading. Peter, however, objects to worksheets, and reasserts the importance of action.

"We should really do it in life," he declares. "We get tired of answering lots of questions. Scientists aren't inside doing worksheets. They're in the world finding things."

"Peter, do scientists write things?" Sue challenges. She would not have done this at the beginning of the year, but mutual trust now permits robust challenges.

"They write after their experiments," says Peter, ignorant of the problems of writing to gain funding for research.

"So you want to write afterwards?"

"We could write lists of what we want to do and then do them and then write it or maybe type it and then tell it," suggests Dan, who a couple of weeks earlier had been resisting any form of writing.

"Sometimes writing things down means you don't forget," says Sue hopefully.

"And you could keep those ideas and that would tell you what children think about," Dan, with something of a "reading problem" and a propensity to rebel if imposed on, recognizes this as an issue. In this discussion he takes the teacher's perspective.

Ann proposes the learning of different sections of a book by different students, who would then teach one another.

"You know what Peter said," bursts Dan. "We don't want to read [about science] all the time. We want to do real things."

Ann is a little startled, and before Sue can think of a way out for her, Evelyn brightly waves the science book all were issued and that they have barely used.

"It gives experiments in your science book."

Everyone takes out their science books. Sue suggests they decide what topics they most want to study. They discuss the book and the issues among themselves. Sue thinks she has a chance to sit for a moment and collect her wits, but quickly people crowd around to say what they are interested in.

"I like animals. I want to be a vet," says Claire with her book open to pictures of animals.

Into the gentle clamor of preferences, Dan brings his review of the textbook. "What do they think we are?" He points to a picture of a calf, with the caption, "What happens if an animal has no food?" "This tells you things I already know. Some of these things my grandfather already told me." His own science books are more complex than the one the book-selection committee has blessed him with.

The bell for recess terminates this flurry of interest and comment. We are delighted and impressed with the class's lively sense of what science is—something they must do, and certainly not a matter of figuring out the answers in the teacher's head. Our project is off to a flying start. We decide to challenge them further.

When they reassemble, Sue asks, "Do you think you will know enough to teach each other?"

"That's not what I mean," says Dan groping for his sense of experiment, discovery, and dialogue. "We could tell each other stuff what we did learn."

"So, you just want to be reporters," says Sue, pushing harder.

"No, no," says Wole. He has said little so far, but senses that Dan and Peter have a more complex case that deserves consideration. "If we're *right*, we can tell people."

"Don't you need a grown-up to tell you if you're right?" Sue persists.

"If you read a book and you're sure it's true, you could tell," another suggests.

"Mrs. Hazzard, you don't get what I'm saying. We can give them information." Dan appears to imply that others can evaluate the information themselves.

"How can *I* tell you got it right?" demands Sue.

"We can prove to you by doing something—like making a light or something. We could do it by attaching wires and showing you."

"Only grown-ups have good ideas," asserts Sue, deadpan, contradicting her everyday practice of taking their ideas seriously.

"Some kids have good ideas," calls Joan.

"Oh, you're trying to get our brains to do brain-work. You're trying to trick us into thinking," Peter accuses.

"I'm really interested . . ." Sue protests. They are both right, but Peter is slightly disgusted.

"You always act like this," he exaggerates.

Ann sees other sides to it. "If you're going to be the teacher, it helps you understand and it helps our friends be able to help each other."

"Know who else it helps?" Dan pauses until everyone looks expectantly at him, then turns to the back of the room. "Dr. Nicholls." They know why Nicholls is here, but the digression is momentary and the show rolls on.

"Other kids can be knowing something a teacher doesn't," claims Joan.

"Since when?" Sue challenges, with a flickering grin.

"Do you know anything about Judo?" says Dan, advancing threateningly, glaring up from just below Sue's waist. Others add their challenges, until Tim, who speaks Armenian, calls, "Teachers don't know Armenian."

"So," says Sue finally, in mock confusion. "So, I don't know everything. That became obvious real quick. Since teachers don't know everything, it wouldn't hurt to share ideas that we know well. And, as you've said, if you don't know things, there are ways we can learn. Remind me of those ways . . ."

They recapitulate their suggestions for methods, and Peter repeats, "Can't we do it in real life?"

"You have my mind swimming with ideas," says Sue. "You want to be explorers and what will I do?"

"Help us."

"Sit round and wait."

"What for?"

"For us to finish."

The children are not unanimous, but the most lively and articulate of them reveal a subtle awareness of what we, the adults in the room, are up to as well as a sense of science as something that they must construct in transactions with the world rather than codified knowledge they must absorb. For Dan, his vociferous supporter Peter, and a good proportion of their classmates, science should be an exploration of the world, and they believe they must check the adequacy of their own knowledge. Sue will lead them to examine these questions further. For the moment, however, provoking them to examine these issues has produced real excitement for the children as well as the adults in the classroom.

In a subsequent free-choice time, Dan enlists a helper and acts on his desire to do experiments. His infectious enthusiasm soon spreads to about half of the class, who abandon their initial math and writing projects to share the book from which he gets his ideas for experiments. But our special interest is in the students' arguments about what science is most worthwhile—in what happens when they are involved in forming the purposes that govern their learning.

INVASION OF THE DINOSAURS

Six weeks after the first discussion of science, in show-and-tell, Dan announces, "These are my dinosaur books and this is my favorite one." He shows several pages, then announces, "This first page is best." He displays a two-page time chart of different species in the periods when they were presumed to live. "See, look at all the details. There are some little animals."

"Why is that little one all by himself?" Peter points to one in a period after most others had become extinct. Sue steps in to hold the book up higher for all to see and to help field the barrage of questions and comments that is swamping Dan. "Why do you think they are nearly all gone later on?"

"Maybe there was war?"

"But were there people back then?"

"No."

"Maybe the book doesn't show all of them."

"Maybe God didn't like them."

"They weren't so intelligent."

Suggestions continue. Students stand at their desks. Some drift to the front.

"Maybe they got smarter and smarter and got to be able to make different kinds."

"God created man after the dinosaurs."

"What if you don't believe in God?" asks Joan. She is rarely impressed by appeals to God or any superior power.

"In the Scriptures it says God created the earth in six days." Evelyn is all earnestness. "On the first day . . ." She receives an attentive audience as she recounts the six days of the creation. Twice when her memory fails, others prompt her. The juxtaposition of evolution and Scripture appears to be accepted as if part of some all-encompassing plan.

"He made man out of woman," Vicki pipes up.

"The other way round," says Vera.

"What about Joan's question? What if you don't believe in God?" asks Sue. "And even if you do, this is a question that's been around for a long time." She begins an account of evolution but quickly leaves it as children press with questions.

"It say here that *Tyrannosaurus rex* was in Indiana [where we are]." Joan has moved to the front and found this in Dan's book.

"Wow!" "Gee!" "Hey!" They break ranks and converge on the book.

Surrounded, the leader goes with the crowd: "From all this I think we'll work up a whole center on dinosaurs." The children studied dinosaurs in the first grade. They know many of their names and something of their habits, but no one is about to claim "We already did this."

"You can write about dinosaurs in your journals," proposes Sue. "Write what you know and what you don't know . . ."

"Can we write our own solutions?" asks Dan.

"Can we use Dan's books?" Tim has a hand on one as he asks.

When Dan and Sue agree, a human wave engulfs the books. Without Sue's bidding, at least half of them sit in pairs reading, talking, and writing about dinosaurs. As Sue unearths more books, these are snapped up.

After 15 minutes, Sue asks what they've come up with. Instead of information, there are questions. "I want to know how long the longest dinosaur is." "How would we survive if dinosaurs were still alive?" "What if they talked?"

"How did they die?" comes up several times.

"Nobody really knows the answer," calls Dan. "But it would be a good one to study."

"I want to say something about Dan," says Paul as the session winds down. "I'm glad he brought the books in 'cause I like things that were a long time ago." A chorus of assent shows he speaks for the majority. So much for the expanding horizons curriculum.

Science lessons rarely focus on the truly unknown, but not because young children can't cope with this form of uncertainty. They know the difference between matters about which we are (for the moment at least) certain and those that are controversial and unsettled and on which teachers have no right to lay down the law (Nicholls & Nelson, 1992). Most of Sue's students are chafing to explore what they know to be unknown.

For part of each day, for a little over a week, dinosaurs are a topic of reading, writing, and discussion.

"Are there any questions we didn't answer?" asks Sue.

"About the longer dinosaurs—how much they ate in one day and, totaling it up, how much they ate in a year?"

"How did they die?" asks Evelyn.

"That's what I want to know."

"So do I."

"That's what everyone wants to know," intones Wole.

"Yes!" cries the chorus.

"If the dinosaurs died," argues Alan, "you're talking about cells and how they change the body. You're talking about how a person would come to life then."

After some discussion, Sue discerns and explains to the others that Alan is asking how humans evolved and are still here and dinosaurs evolved but aren't still here.

"Some people believe God made dinosaurs and some don't." This is a variant of one of Joan's favorite themes—"If you didn't believe in God . . ." But she has another puzzle now. "I thought they came from little to big so they can't come from big to little. People would have to be first."

Size increase among dinosaurs is discussed extensively.

Peter focuses on within-group diversity. "You know how dinosaurs changed kinds. So did men. I'm just saying dinosaurs changed and so do we. One man couldn't be all the kinds there are so we must have changed."

Alan suggests that the sun makes people different colors. Ann returns to species transformations.

"I think if man is brought by animals, then birds must be from pterodactyls."

"No! Not pterodactyl." Vicki is a pterodactyl lover and expert. "It has rubbery skin and wings."

Joan brings to the front Dan's chart indicating time periods when different dinosaurs predominated. She discusses it with Sue and the crowd that grows round them. Sue draws the less loquacious students into the discussion. She points out that Joan has detected similarities in dinosaurs from different time periods.

"What is similar about these ones, Paul?" she points to *Triceratops* and similar creatures, which appear in several time periods.

"They have shields and horns."

Sue continues round the class, drawing in everyone. Then, out of the blue, Paul raises the question of authority in science.

"That [chart] says *Stegosaurus* and *Tyrannosaurus rex* were in different times, but the film [from the day before] showed they fought each other."

"Which is right?" says Sue who had been waiting for a chance to ask "How do we know what to believe?"

"People who write books, they don't write things about things that aren't right. There is more in a book that we know is real," says Dan, owner of the book.

"Books say exactly and a movie says 'maybe,'" offers Joan.

"So if it's written in a book, it must always be true?"

"No!" they cry.

"They'll tell you if a book is make-believe," says Joan.

"Books don't always tell the truth," says Vera.

"How can you tell if they do?"

"You see if it makes sense," answers Vera. Perhaps she is groping for a thought expressed by William James (1907):

> That ideas (which themselves are but parts of our experience) become true just in so far as they help us get into satisfactory relation with other parts of our experience. (p. 58)

James's pragmatist approach to truth does not satisfy everyone, but it is hard to improve on. Sue, however, persists: "How do we know if something doesn't make sense?"

"You can tell," claims Joan. "Like if you write 'Joan' with an *i* [instead of *o*] you can see it doesn't make sense."

Murmurs of doubt are heard, and Joan nods agreement when Dan says, "There's lots of Johnsons, and I've come to realize that they're not all spelled the same." The students recognize the arbitrary nature of the conventions of spelling and see that these are not established in the same way as substantive claims (Nicholls & Thorkildsen, 1989).

"Sometimes," says Vera, clarifying her position, "you can tell 'cause if it tells you something you know isn't true, you know to not believe."

"You can look in different books like the dictionary," adds Jack.

"So, if it's in the dictionary, is it true?"

"Books usually have labels that tell you whether it's make-believe or nonfiction. Fiction is what's make-believe so nonfiction is real." Peter's logic seems to satisfy him fully.

"So this book is nonfiction. So is it or the video right?" challenges Sue.

"I went to the book shop, to the history books, to the 'for sure' books," says Dan. "If they get the books scrambled up, it's their fault."

Ann raises the author's motives. "Maybe the person who wrote it wanted to be right when they were little and when they grew up they learned the way it really was. Then they would know."

"I think the book is true," proposes Claire, "because the video might be old and the book is newer."

Though eager to battle on exploring variations of their suggestions, they are unable to progress much more.

"So," asks Sue, urging them to reflect on their purposes, "why are people interested in dinosaurs?"

"Because it's an unknown thing, like an adventure," says Dan.

"So, if it's unknown, it's more interesting?"

"Just like space," he says.

"It's like we're guessing," chimes Joan.

"Like scientists!" calls Vicki waving her arm, as if being a scientist is like being one of the Three Musketeers. She has followed the discussion while flipping through a dinosaur book, appearing not to be engaged. But when she detects a problem (about the evolution of birds, for example) or a point that needs enhancement, she is wholly focused, deftly inserting her contribution into the mosaic of discussion.

"First we're reading the books and then we're guessing and then we see if we're right," says Joan.

"It'd be more of an adventure if we could find out on our own." Dan repeats his theme.

After a digression on *Stegosaurs*, Peter again supports Dan. "Like Dan was saying, I think we should go out and dig and see what we find."

Others doubt the advisability of ruining "our yard" and ask, "Where are the tools?"

"I don't think it was a real *Tyrannosaurus rex*," says Paul, returning to the videotape, "so I don't believe the movie."

"Why?"

"'Cause dinosaurs can't be around."

"Turtles are dinosaurs and they're around," says Alan.

"So why did big ones die and not the little ones?"

"They could have fought, and the little ones kept safe, and the big ones killed each other," Ann suggests.

"There is big turtles still alive," says Alan. His eyes are popping with determination to communicate the enormity of the one he saw at a zoo. "It could eat one whole banana . . . at . . . probably," his eyes roll, "two bites."

"The big ones died because when you get old you die," suggests Claire, apparently confusing age and size of individuals with evolution and size of species.

Suggestions flow.

"Maybe the big ones' brains were not so smart," proposes Vicki. "And the little ones were smarter."

"I read a book that said the little ones didn't have big brains," says Dan.

The possibility of climatic change is raised. They refer to different books they read that implicated both higher and lower temperatures.

"What if it got hot?" asks Sue.

"Maybe they get sweaty and plants would grow more. And they could get burned. Maybe their skin was light like mine," wonders Vicki.

"Maybe they die when they get sweaty," says Jack.

"Maybe they aren't extinct. Turtles and jellyfish are alive. Maybe it's the land ones that died," says Peter.

"So only the land ones disappeared?"

"But there were water dinosaurs that died," Peter recalls, changing his mind.

"Maybe a comet hits the earth and spins it round and the animals spin off and fall back broken so only little ones are left." Jodie gestures to evoke this disaster. "Maybe that's how those rocks in space [asteroids, which they had studied earlier] came."

"They could have frozen in space," says Wole.

"Cold and snow killed them." Jack holds up a book showing dying dinosaurs in snow.

"So how could it get cold?" asks Sue.

"The rings of Saturn are made of ice," says Peter. "If comets can flash by the earth, perhaps Saturn or its rings can?"

Hot versus cold and their effects are discussed. Ann suggests, "Plants could die, plant eaters die, and meat eaters have no food so . . ."

The possibility that the earth's water could have evaporated, how evaporation happens, and its probable effects are explored.

"If something rushes past you fast, it makes a cold wind," says Tim, working to bring part of his experience "into satisfactory relation with other parts."

They discuss the effects climatic changes would have, what colors the dinosaurs were, and then, back to evolution.

"If there was no changing cells, we'd all be the same," claims Alan.

"The Bible doesn't say that." Jack is authoritative. His back is straight, his expression firm.

"So the Bible tells us the whole answer?" asks Sue.

"Yes!" Jack is determined, "Because God made the whole earth."

"If people came from animals," says Ann, pursuing Alan's theme, "and we are from Indiana where *Tyrannosaurus rex* was, we'd have some of *Tyrannosaurus rex*'s blood."

"Claire, what do you think?"

"Man came from God."

"Where did the animals come from?"

"From Jesus. I believe in Jesus."

"I'm confused. God and Jesus made different things? I thought they both made all the same things?" Joan presents this as a question, but her manner gently implies that Claire's idea makes no sense.

"It says in the Bible . . ." Peter begins, but Joan cuts him off firmly.

"It never said he made dinosaurs."

"But he made *all* the animals and dinosaurs are animals so," Peter strikes back, "*unfortunately*, you are wrong." This is the only moment in this hour and a half of discussion when a touch of personal venom appears.

Jack is adamant about God's role and accepts no challenges. He says he has seen dinosaurs in a book about how God made the earth. But he bears no animosity toward the Darwinians and Lamarkians of the class. He assumes that natural explanations can also be valid. He follows and contributes robustly to discussions on these matters—now championing the ice age theory, then arguing another position.

"How did the first dinosaur get on earth?" James is earnest. God's act seems an incomplete explanation for him.

"God made the animals and the people. They were made separate, at different times."

"Who believes God made the dinosaurs and everything else?" asks Sue. Every hand, Joan's included, goes up.

"So how would a person who doesn't believe in God explain all the dinosaurs and animals?"

"I know what you're doing." Peter stands up pointing at Sue. "You're trying to get us to think. This is not doing us any good except to get us ready to think hard." What indeed is he thinking? We are both puzzled by his earnest and emotional challenge.

"Is it good to get you to think hard and maybe change your mind?" asks Sue, but the class is too interested in thinking hard to answer Sue's question.

"They say there's no dinosaurs left. How do they know?" Paul questions urgently, once again bringing up this question. "How do they really know?"

"Yes," chimes Peter, who is suddenly hard to recognize as the person who just questioned the value of thinking hard. "How *do* we know?"

"Some things *look* like they were a long time ago," Vera suggests.

"You saw on the film how some scientists put together a dinosaur's bones and years later someone found they had the wrong head on it. How could they know that?"

"By the imprints in different parts of the bones," says Peter, who seems unable to stop thinking hard.

"They could have another and it looked better on it," proposes Evelyn.

"They saw that the head of the new one could go on it," adds Paul.

The bell for the end of school rings. There is no sign of flagging interest. The questions about what is worth knowing, and how we check our knowledge coexist easily with attempts to know more about dinosaurs. There is little sense that answers to any of these questions are in the teacher's head, waiting to be transmitted to the students' heads. Taking her lead from Paul's question, Sue proposes that tonight they should think about how you know when you are right about something and how scientists know when they are right.

WHO KNOWS? AND DOES THE JOURNEY END?

The next day, the suggestion that you can tell whether a claim is correct by asking experts makes sense to several speakers, but Peter will not hear of it.

"Their source is not your source. You need to *do* things. You need to go to your sources, not their sources." He is passionate in his demand that one's knowledge in science should not rest on faith in experts. Some others are not persuaded. Sue refocuses the discussion:

"Who is an expert?"

"Scientists."

"My grandpa is an expert at woodwork."

"How do you become an expert?" asks Sue.

"God is an expert," contributes Evelyn.

"He was already an expert," adds Vera.

Yesterday Dan implied that if you got the right type of book, what it said would be true. Today he was ready to rely on experts. Now he has second thoughts. He recounts a visit to a doctor who "never gave us any medicine, so we had to go to a better doctor. Scientists seem like they're rich and know everything, but they don't."

"You can't know everything," contributes Peter. "There are some things people can't know. It's been proven that we can't know everything."

Others reassert the limits of knowledge until Sue asks, "Should scientists give up?"

"No, they just keep trying."

"Some things you think are impossible you can do if you just keep on trying."

"Like bringing dinosaurs back to life? You can't do that," qualifies Dan.

"Does science ever stop?"

"No, it can't. Like a hundred years ago, maybe they didn't know about dinosaurs," says Dan.

"Why?"

"Maybe they didn't have the stuff for digging them."

"Like the guy who invented the telephone. . . . People said you couldn't talk like that, and he made a thing like a record and an earphone and he talked through it. I don't know how." She does, however, know that the incomprehensible might eventually be comprehended and the impossible be made possible.

The conversation returns to how you know if you are right.

"You study on it," Alan offers.

"How?"

"Use tools," he suggests.

"You use your brain. You think and figure it out for yourself," calls Vicki.

"It's like a big mystery to scientists," declares Alan. "It's like a big maze you have to find your way through."

"It's like you're this small and trying to drive a bumper car and can't reach the pedal," suggests little Tim.

They get back to diversity of scientific opinion.

"What you get most of is the best one," proposes Dan.

"It's like voting," chimes Vera.

"Can you make the wrong decision voting?" asks Sue, but the specific intervenes again as Peter goes to the globe and suggests that one could check the theory of continental drift by cutting up a map and seeing if the pieces fit. A number vow to look at home for maps so they could try this.

Timid Martha must have been reflecting on Alan's maze metaphor because she now tries to relate the mirror maze on the television program "Double Dare" to the discussion.

"No," says Wole, "Alan is thinking of the maze that's in Fun House."

"I meant," says Alan, after Sue questions him, "that you can't find all the answers. There are bits you can't find."

Peter elaborates the metaphor. "It's like there's lots of doors and as soon as you get the information, it fits together and you've got a key and it opens a door and you go through and there's another door. When you get to the last door, you know it all."

"Are we there?" Sue asks.

A enthusiastic chorus of "No!" leaves no doubt how much they relish the idea of science as a never-ending quest.

William James (1907) wrote, "When the first mathematical, logical, and natural uniformities, the first *laws*, were discovered, men were so carried away by the clearness, beauty and simplification that resulted, that they believed themselves to have deciphered authentically the eternal thoughts of the Almighty" (p. 56). James hinted that this notion was passing, and he hoped it was. But the idea that science is most truly science and most to be revered when it reveals eternal truths, unstained by human biases, is still with us. Many students and faculty of the physical sciences see their disciplines as superior to others, not because they provide endless and exciting quests but because of the abstractness and impersonality of their formulations and the precision of their predictions, methods, and findings.

Such contemporary expressions of what Dewey called the quest for certainty are a far cry from this second-grade quest for excitement. These children seem closer to the spirit of James's (1907) notion that "no theory is absolutely a transcript of reality . . . only a man-made language, a conceptual shorthand . . . in which we write our reports of nature; and languages, as is well known, tolerate much choice of expression and many dialects" (p. 57).

"In the Europe of the 16th century, as in classical Athens, some scholars condemned as irrational *con*fusion what others welcomed as intellectual *pro*fusion" (Toulmin, 1990, p. 27). Most of our second-graders revel in profusion. They align themselves with those who see science as a messy, human affair. They have no fear of a profusion of ideas. They are ready, with Montaigne and the Renaissance humanists, "to suspend judgment about matters of general theory, and to concentrate on accumulating a rich perspective, both on the natural world and on human affairs, as we encounter them" (Toulmin, 1990, p. 27). At least they are ready to do this when the topics are ones they see as controversial—topics such as the evolution and extinction of dinosaurs or the existence of witches.

WHANGDOODLES, WITCHES, AND KNOWLEDGE

Early in May, Sue started reading *The Last of the Really Great Whangdoodles* (Edwards, 1974). The definition of *whangdoodle* in the students' dictionaries proves confusing: "'noun, slang: a fanciful creature of undefined nature.'" They turn to a larger dictionary from the library, which presents new problems.

"What's *mythical*?" asks Wole.

They discuss *mythical*, *fanciful*, and *undefined*.

This stimulates a story from Jodie about a ghostly house.

"Was Redeye in there?" Jack wants to know.

"There's no such thing as Redeye."

"Who knows? Who knows?" Jack advances across the room, loftily and firmly, his finger pointing at the doubting Joan. "He's a ghost!"

"Are there ghosts?" asks Sue.

A conglomeration of yes's and no's erupts.

"And there *are* witches!" Jack is firm. "On the radio I heard a witch talking to the man."

"How did you know it was a witch?"

"I heard on the radio, and they said on the radio that their pure washing color is red."

"When they wash . . . ?" Sue prompts.

"They put blood in it."

"I don't believe it a bit," explodes Joan.

"I've got evidence on ghosts," claims Tim. "I saw it on the news and I was in the audience. The guy was talking to the man and some kind of blob came behind him. It looked gooey and red. I'm not sure if it was red, but I think it was."

"Where were you?"

"In the audience."

"Where?"

"In the theater."

"Is it Paul?" asks Jack.

"No. They were broadcasting."

"He's making it up."

"You never know 'cause maybe it's a regular person."

"How can you tell it's a witch 'cause it's on the radio and you can't see?"

"This was a Christian radio station and Christians can't lie 'cause they'll break a law." Jack is resolute.

"Do they ever lie?" asks Sue.

"Sometimes, but not at this radio station 'cause they were face to face with a real witch."

Peter distinguishes truth from the experience of certainty: "Yourself, you can be sure but you can't be positive."

"Yeah! It might be that. He can say that, but he can't prove it. How do you know they are really there? Do you have a crystal ball?"

Jack bursts with moral indignation. "A crystal ball is *evil magic*! I don't have a crystal ball. I wouldn't!"

"Does anyone believe, as Jack does, that there are witches and ghosts?" A third of the class raise their hands.

"It was moving across the stage," says Tim.

"There was wheels under it," suggests Joan.

"It was floating. I could see the bottom." Their enthusiasm to offer interpretations overwhelms the normal turn-taking. When calm is restored, Sue calls on Elizabeth.

"It might be someone dressed up like in the movies. People pull them through the air with strings."

"A movie projection."

"They are pretending."

"They sounded like a real witch." Jack is determined. He speaks loudly, but not vindictively. "Okay," he challenges, striding to the front of the room. "Everyone try to talk like a witch and I'll tell you if it's real."

"People can tell lies as easily as the truth," proposes Evelyn.

"So, do you think Tim and Jack are lying?" asks Sue.

The class is divided.

"How do you [Tim and Jack] know they weren't just tricking you?" asks Evelyn.

"So they could be telling the truth, but the people tricked them?" checks Sue. Evelyn nods to this, but wants stronger evidence from Jack:

"If a witch turned him into a frog and he came hopping in here, then I might believe it."

Wole has found *witch* in the dictionary. "It's someone who practices magic," he offers.

"There's no such thing as magic."

"There is!"

"No!"

"It's just tricks."

"You think you're seeing it and you're not. It's not doing what they think."

"It could be a hologram."

"Holograms are just pictures from a special projector," says Tim.

"Yes, but three-dimensional," adds Dan.

Jack has found *witch* in the dictionary. "It says a witch is an ugly old woman, especially," he points at the unbelievers, "of an *evil* nature." Other dictionary definitions are offered without resolution of the questions.

Martha believes there could be ghosts because she just heard a ghostly singing in the corridor. (Later she will confide to Sue that she discovered it was the fourth-graders downstairs practicing for a concert.)

Sue moves to conclude. "I think we found people who have strong ideas and no one has given enough proof to change other people's ideas. This happens often in life. What should we do in situations like this—when someone believes the opposite of you and they won't change?"

"Nothing."

"Ask someone else."

"Let them believe what they want to."

"Yes. There's no way you can change their belief."

"Jack, you presented a strong argument," recalls Sue. "Are you trying to prove it for them or to convince yourself?"

"I already know. I've got proof!"

"Is anyone not sure about this?" About one-third of them raise their hands.

"You don't have to believe," suggests Joan. "It's like the president. Some people don't like the president we have. But they choose." Not only does she resist blind appeals to higher authority; she holds that decisions about truth must be left to fallible humans who must live with diversity.

Sue concludes with the suggestion Dan made in the first discussion of science: If we listen to others, something they say might make sense. Though always animated and occasionally intense, the discussion has been tolerant. It has created no enemies. Jack was very assertive, and at times under siege. Though he, more than anyone, claimed certainty, he never stooped to personal attack and he listened to his classmates. He shows no sign of having dismissed his peers or of having himself been diminished. Indeed, he is energized.

DIVERSITY AND ADVENTURE OR THE QUEST FOR CERTAINTY?

Generally, students in our schools come to assume that scientific knowledge is a collection of facts, rules, and laws to be memorized rather than constructed in personal and social inquiry. This, and the failure of a majority of students to comprehend the science lessons they have apparently been studying, has been of some national concern (National Assessment of Educational Progress, 1979).

It might be that science educators have inadvertently got what some of them wanted. "Problem solving in a domain such as physics has," according to two who study science education, "the advantage of having 'real-world' features and of being associated with a *well-structured* knowledge domain (principles of physics) and *well-defined* problem-solving procedures. These *attractive features* have led to a cumulative, systematic research effort in physics and mathematics problem-solving" (Eylon & Linn, 1988, p. 237; emphasis added). If learning science is primarily a matter of acquiring well-structured knowledge and unambiguously right answers, it is unlikely to be an adventure. It is more likely to become the quest for the one right answer in the teacher's head.

Science can sweep aside intellectual fogs. Yet science also seeks and creates puzzles, paradoxes, and controversy. In basic biomedical research, writes Lewis Thomas (1974),

> what you need at the outset is a high degree of uncertainty: otherwise it isn't likely to be an important problem. . . . There are fascinating ideas all over the place, irresistible experiments beyond numbering, all sorts of new ways into the maze of problems. But every next move is unpredict-

able, every outcome uncertain. It is a puzzling time, but a very good time. (pp. 118–119)

Jodie and her classmates are not old enough to understand fully that to determine whether a given variable produces a given effect, one must control for the effects of other variables. In this sense, they do not understand what an experiment is (Piaget, 1972). If we emphasize this, they will all look like inferior scientists. Yet Jodie and many of her peers are wholeheartedly with Thomas when he presents science as an intellectual adventure. If this is the heart of science, they are scientists at heart.

The uncertainty-reducing function of science gets most of the playing time in schools and in research on science education. Perhaps this is why, as Thomas (1982) puts it, "the worst thing that has happened to science education is that the fun has gone out of it" (p. 93). "We might begin looking more closely at the common ground that science shares with . . . the humanities and with social and behavioral science. For there is such a common ground. It is called bewilderment" (p. 91). "Leave the so-called basics aside for a while, and concentrate the attention of all students on the things that are not known" (p. 92).

Even first-graders recognize that there are many phenomena about which we are pretty certain. A spacecraft, for example, will not float up from earth unassisted into orbit. They also recognize areas where disagreement is endemic and legitimate. Is there, for example, life elsewhere in space? (Nicholls & Nelson, 1992). When science is a matter of acquiring "well-structured," absolute knowledge, children can be wrong, stupid, and reluctant to explore every day of the year. But, given the right conditions, controversial topics strike no fear into these would-be scientists with licenses to guess and to travel in exciting mazes without end.

But our second-grade scientists and science educators have taught us more. They have made manifest the ability to doubt and to respect others that Jacob Bronowski (1973) hoped science would deliver:

> It is said that science will dehumanize people and turn them into numbers. That is false, tragically false. . . . [I am standing at] the . . . crematorium at Auschwitz. This is where people were turned into numbers. . . . It was done by dogma. . . . When people believe they have absolute knowledge, with no test in reality, this is how they behave. This is what men do when they aspire to the knowledge of gods.
>
> Science is a very human form of knowledge . . . every judgment in science stands on the edge of error, and is personal. Science is a tribute to what we can know although we are fallible. In the end, the words were said by Oliver Cromwell: "I beseech you, in the bowels of Christ, think it possible you may be mistaken."

> I . . . stand here at Auschwitz [where members of my family died] as a
> survivor and a witness. We have to cure ourselves of the itch for absolute
> knowledge and power. . . . We have to touch people. (p. 374)

We should not cast a too rosy light on all this. Threats to Bronowski's
vision remain in Sue's class. Peter, for example, ardent intellectual ad-
venturer, articulate exponent of science as "what you're thinking about
and what you discover," also worries that he is only learning to think
hard and not absorbing enough information. As they contemplate the
unknown terrors of the third grade, he and some of the others fear that
they have not accumulated enough noncontroversial facts to help them
survive the tests that lie ahead. The state and the school system cursed
Sue and her students with two time-consuming standardized achievement
tests during the year. Nowhere in these tests were there any questions
like "Why did the dinosaurs die out?" "Did God have anything to do with
the rise and fall of the dinosaurs?" or "Are there witches?" It is hardly
surprising that questions about the unknown can seem irrelevant when
test scores are important. As the third grade approaches, some of those
who thrilled to inquire about controversial matters reach for the cold
comfort of "testable" knowledge.

Yet we remain impressed with the students' zest for the unknown,
and their readiness to hold their own truths questionable. Somehow, out
of these explorations into dinosaurs, space, witches, and whangdoodles,
Bronowski's lesson emerged for most of them. We could hardly have
hoped for more.

It is hard to see how all this could happen without involving students in the formation of the purposes that govern their activities. Sue's
readiness to stop "giving a lesson" on evolution when she saw the students wanted to pose their own questions, allowed them essential
space. In a climate of mutual respect, her challenging questions and
their challenges to each other provoked the intelligent formation of
purposes, of reasons for learning. Our second-graders' vigorous conversations about science are explorations of reasons for doing science,
of ways of living as scientists. This is the making of the curriculum and
the making of the curriculum is not separable from the making of reasons for learning. When Dan passionately declares, then acts on his
desire to do experiments, we hear and see his reasons for learning—his
motivation. As these reasons evolve and are acted out, so is his curriculum. For teachers as well as students, this means that education is not
a ride to a preassigned destination, but a communal, adventurous journey to places yet unknown—a journey that requires tolerance for others' questions as well as their answers.

REFERENCES

Boomer, G., Lester, N., Onore, C., & Cook, J. (Eds.). (1992). *Negotiating the curriculum: Educating for the 21st Century.* London: Falmer.

Bronowski, J. (1973). *The ascent of man.* London: British Broadcasting Corporation.

Dewey, J. (1938). *Experience and education.* New York: Macmillan.

Goodlad, J. I. (1983). *A place called school: Prospects for the future.* New York: McGraw-Hill.

Edwards, J. (1974). *The last of the really great whangdoodles.* New York: Harper & Row.

Erickson, F., & Shultz, J. (1992). Students' experience of the curriculum. In P. W. Jackson (Ed.), *Handbook of research on curriculum* (pp. 465–485). New York: Macmillan.

Eylon, B.-S., & Linn, M. C. (1988). Learning and instruction: An examination of four research perspectives in science education. *Review of Educational Research, 58,* 251–301.

James, W. (1907). *Pragmatism: A new name for some old ways of thinking.* New York: Longmans, Green, and Co.

Korn, C. V. (1991). *Alternative American schools.* Albany: State University of New York Press.

Mayhew, K. C., & Edwards, A. C. (1936). *The Dewey school: The laboratory school of the University of Chicago.* New York: Appleton-Century. (Atherton Press edition, 1965)

National Assessment of Educational Progress. (1979). *Attitudes toward science: A summary of results from the 1976–77 national assessment of science.* (Report No. 08-S-02). Denver, CO: Education Commission of the States.

Nicholls, J. G., & Hazzard, S. P. (1993). *Education as adventure: Lessons from the second grade.* New York: Teachers College Press.

Nicholls, J. G., & Nelson, J. R. (1992). Students' conceptions of controversial knowledge. *Journal of Educational Psychology, 84,* 224–230.

Nicholls, J. G., & Thorkildsen, T. A. (1989). Intellectual conventions versus matters of substance: Elementary school students as curriculum theorists. *American Educational Research Journal, 26,* 533–544.

Piaget, J. (1972). Intellectual evolution from adolescence to adulthood. *Human Development, 15,* 1–12.

Thomas, L. (1974). *The lives of a cell: Notes of a biology watcher.* New York: Viking.

Thomas, L. (1982, March 14). The art of teaching science. *New York Times Magazine,* pp. 89–93.

Toulmin, S. (1990). *Cosmopolis: The hidden agenda of modernity.* New York: The Free Press.

7 Is There a Right Way to Collaborate?

WHEN THE EXPERTS SPEAK, CAN THE CUSTOMERS BE RIGHT?

Theresa A. Thorkildsen, University of Illinois at Chicago
Candace Jordan, Milwaukee Public Schools

Students with Candace Jordan

Worried about the motivation of some of her students, Candace Jordan turned to cooperative learning research for guidance. She and her students tried out and critiqued the common practice of assigning students to groups. They discovered that this practice ignores the importance of trust, mood, and friendship in genuine collaboration. Together, students and teacher learned to seek responsiveness rather than tolerance, and communicated experience rather than consensus. They invented a scholarly community that respects the motivation of all its members. Many of the formal cooperative learning models, in their view, fail to value (and in some cases explicitly undermine) long-term relationships. Finding the right way to collaborate will forever remain a controversial moral task.

137

Candace Jordan, a teacher of fourth- and fifth-graders, invited Terri Thorkildsen, an assistant professor, to help her improve the quality of collaboration in her classroom. Candace had heard about seminars on cooperative learning, put on by Johnson and Johnson (1989) or their associates, that suggested the "correct" approach and wondered if her spontaneously generated methods could be improved upon. Leery of anything declared to be "correct" by the very researchers who are "selling" it, Candace decided to skip the seminars and, instead, read about a variety of cooperative learning methods. Then, because she and I shared a faith that children have "the capacity for intelligent judgment and action if proper conditions are furnished" (Dewey, 1940, p. 224), we elicited the help of her students in our inquiry about fair and effective ways to collaborate.

A NONTRADITIONAL CLASSROOM

September 27. Candace's room was originally two classrooms, now joined to make a large one. There are two bird cages, a plant corner, a science area, and an art corner, complete with well-stocked supply cabinets. Spread throughout the room are four large tables with chairs and many small clusters of desks and chairs. A large rug in the center is used for class meetings and to allow students space comfortably to spread out their work. The walls are virtually empty. "This is the students' room. They will spend the year filling those walls with interesting work," Candace tells me.

Of the twenty-four 9- to 11-year-olds, 15 are girls and 9 are boys. About half are African-American; the balance are European-American, Latin-American, or have dual ethnicity. Half are fourth-graders who are new to Candace's room and the other half are fifth-graders who were with her last year.[1]

On my first visit, a calm hum fills the room. Students work on different tasks, some in groups, others alone. Bernadette, who looks like a teenager, is deeply engrossed in a romance novel. I comment on her obvious enjoyment. She tries to read on, but answers my questions politely. Sheloanda and DeAndre seem tiny and light years away from puberty. They are side by side eyeing the computer screen. Proud of their work but eager to get back to it, they tell me that they are writing science fiction. They quickly page through the document to show that they have

This paper was presented at the annual conference of the Association for Moral Education, Toronto, Canada, November 1992.

already written several chapters. "We're going to fill the whole disk," they say and, ignoring me, continue chattering about the story.

Most of the others are working in small groups making book-like reports about the universe. One group is comparing the perspectives of different authors and discussing possible chapters for their reports. Should there be one for each planet? What about galaxies? As they talk, students write, in their own words, the ideas that they think are important, on 1 inch by 8½-inch strips of paper. Copying from books, they tell me, is not allowed for these reports.

Latoya wants help with a word and invites me into her group. Some of these students, like workers on a production line, doggedly count the number of slips they have written and show little interest in the ideas. Others are excited by the ideas they discover and even distract themselves from writing. When classmates ask how many slips they have written, the production line workers are ready with tallies, but the explorers have to count. Furthermore, the explorers spontaneously tally the number of slips accumulated by the whole group, whereas the production line workers tally their individual contributions.

Another group had, over previous days, done what the class calls "research," and accumulated enough ideas on slips to begin organizing their report. On the carpet, they sort their strips into themes. Others translate the previously organized piles of slips into text, while the artists among them illustrate the emerging story.

Mathew, Emmet, and Angela are practicing spelling words. They stop to show me a book of poems to which each had contributed. The three chatter about each poem—when and why it was written and who drew what. They note their favorite parts, compliment one another's work, and occasionally criticize or revise. Mathew and Angela bicker amiably about whose turn it is to read the book, revealing that they daily take turns rereading and editing it.

"We have so many ideas [for poems]," Mathew declares, "that we are starting a second book." Mathew and Angela dig in their desks to find their artwork for the new cover.

Instead, Mathew brings out his finished report on the universe. Neatly written and illustrated paragraphs describe each planet and the origin of the universe. He included puzzles "to make it fun to read," an introduction about why knowledge about the universe is important, a cover and title page, and a section about the author.

"Emmet helped me with the drawing. He's a really good artist," notes Mathew, and Emmet beams.

Most students show similar pride in their reports. Although they construct individual reports, there is no question that each one bears the fruit of collaboration. Collaboration is spontaneous and the group compositions change often. As a result, good ideas spread slowly throughout the class. Sometimes the originators are credited, other times they are not. By the time other universe books are complete, for example, Mathew's idea of adding a section called, "About the Author," is included in many of them. Mathew got his idea from the covers of books, but he wrote his own version, including a statement about why he finds the topic interesting—his reasons for learning. He wouldn't think of claiming "credit" for the idea, nor did he feel cheated when his classmates imitated him. Students saw imitation as the sharing of ideas, not as cheating.

INSIGHTS FROM COOPERATIVE LEARNING THEORY

This struck me as a nearly ideal collaborative community of scholars, yet Candace was worried about some of the more marginal members. Debbie, for example, was seen as bossy by many of the other students, and she disliked working with them. Sharmon had a limited tolerance for frustration and a violent temper that frightened others. Sheloanda used the freedom to choose as an excuse to avoid schoolwork. Bringing frustrations from home, DeAndre would hurt at least one child before settling in for what was often a productive day. Candace wanted to prevent these students from becoming permanently rejected and hoped the academic research on cooperative learning could help.

Rather than suddenly and dramatically change the way students did their reports, Candace thought we should gradually incorporate the specific practices endorsed by cooperative learning theorists. We began by assigning students to groups, a practice recommended by many researchers (e.g., Johnson & Johnson, 1975, 1989; Sharan, 1980; Sharan, Kussel, Hertz-Lazarowitz, Bejarano, Raviv, & Sharan, 1984; Slavin, 1983, 1991a). According to Johnson & Johnson (1975), for example, students should be assigned to groups with "a good mixture of boys and girls, highly verbal and passive students, leaders and followers, and enthusiastic and reluctant learners" (pp. 91–92). Researchers prefer this method because, as in Candace's class, when students are allowed to choose collaborators, some would be isolated and their learning would suffer.

Each group, it is commonly held, needs to have an initial reason to cohere and form a collective identity (e.g., Johnson & Johnson, 1975; Slavin, 1983). For this reason, Candace asked students to choose a leader and a name for their group.

Most researchers also argue that incentives are needed to induce collaboration. Teachers, they say, can use extrinsic rewards (Johnson &

Johnson, 1975; Sharan et al., 1984; Slavin, 1991b) or ask groups to complete a single report that would be evaluated according to a predetermined set of standards (Johnson & Johnson, 1975, p. 132). The use of special rewards was blatantly against the philosophy of education advocated at MacDowell.[2] Candace saw such extrinsic incentives as the "bench of the soul, the instrument of slavery for the spirit" (Montessori, 1965, p. 21). She was aware of the corrosive effect of rewards on intrinsic interest in learning (Lepper & Greene, 1978). Her students did not receive such rewards or grades, and this would not change.

Candace would also not adopt Johnson & Johnson's (1975) suggestion of predetermined standards. That notion presumes there is a universal, content-free definition of a "good report," and that all intellectual quests end at known destinations. Predetermined standards would restrict students' ability to form their own purposes for learning and to convey their interests. There would be little room for surprises and insight. Therefore, members of each group collaborated on a single, written report. Yet Candace encouraged them to express their findings in innovative and personally meaningful ways, a practice consistent with only one of the cooperative learning models we looked at (Sharan et al., 1984).

We agreed with Bowles and Gintis (1976) and Dewey (1916/1944), who claim that democracy should be extended to all parts of social life. In most schools, as in the world of work, democratic participation of any sort is nonexistent. Contrary to this norm, Candace regularly included students in discussions of classroom rules, discipline problems, and plans for field trips and parties. Her practices were consistent with much of what is done in Kohlberg's Just Community programs, where students make rules to regulate personal conduct and solve discipline problems (e.g., Power, Higgins, & Kohlberg, 1989). In both contexts, however, democratic participation had been limited—students were not asked to govern their learning. They had not been encouraged to serve as educational theorists who negotiate their academic purposes and critique practices intended to promote intellectual growth.

We hoped to remedy this by asking Candace's students to reflect on the ways in which they collaborate. We hoped that by critiquing their experiences, students would see room for improvement and accept our idea of assigned groups.

October 10. Candace and her students sit in a circle. She asks individuals to speak only when holding a tape recorder, which they hand around like the conch in *Lord of the Flies*. The tone is more solemn than is common for class council meetings.

"How did you decide who to work with today?" Candace begins.

"By how they act."

"And how they work."

"If they like to make distractions, then I don't work with them."

"Sometimes I get a funny feeling that I would like to work with some person."

"OK, some of you are saying if you get along with them, and some of you are saying if you get a funny feeling. Now think about that funny feeling. How many of you can put into words what that funny feeling is? What are some of the things that you look for—that direct you?"

"They cooperate," says Lavar who frequently leaves a group if things don't go his way.

Latoya elaborates, "Like if they doing some math, and then they get up and go somewhere else, then you wouldn't work with them."

The conversation continues on this bland note for some time. Candace encourages students to think more deeply about their decisions, but students are initially reluctant to critique their learning experiences. They nervously wiggle and admit that this is difficult. Candace persists and, sensing her serious interest, the students start giving more details.

"I don't like to work with people who is gonna try to take over the report, and people that's gonna think that they know everything, and well . . ." says Jamika.

"Do you like working with groups most or by yourself most of the time?" asks Candace.

"I mostly like working by myself because I can be in charge of this project and there's no one who can get snotty to me," asserts domineering Debbie. "But sometimes it's nice working in groups because you get the job done faster and you make friends easier."

"I don't like working in groups," states Gary, "because I like having my own report so I could just feel good about myself and not others."

"I like working in groups because sometimes, like if you get stuck on a math problem, then you have somebody to help you—figure it out with you," chimes Latoya, who never seems embarrassed to ask for help.

"Well sometimes when you do the report you feel good about yourself and *you're* the one that's getting the credit." Jamika agrees with Gary.

"I like to work in groups because I make friends and it's really easier. Because I feel good about myself and I feel like everybody that worked with me should feel good about theirself, too," asserts Mathew.

"I don't like working in groups," says Monique, "because when you make a report, and they only make a little slips and you worked hard on it, and they made only about two or three slips and you made a lot, then it's not fair."

"If you need help you won't have to go to the teacher all the time, you can go to your friend," says Deetra.

"I like working with people," says Dionne, who is consistently helped by others. "'Cause if they don't know something, I could help them. And, if I don't know something, they could help me."

"If you don't have a friend, you don't know what you're missing because friends are the best thing in the world," claims Chantal, who values friendship in its own right.

This comment strikes Jamika, who previously said that she prefers to work alone. She now claims, "I like working with nice people because nice people, they don't always get attitudes and start yelling at you, 'I want to do this. I want to write this.'"

"You should work *for* people," asserts Monique, returning to Chantal's communal theme.

In addition to more general comments about the need for hard work and polite behavior, these children differ in the extent to which they assert competitive, individualistic, and communal themes—themes that influence whether and with whom they choose to collaborate. Those who think in terms of receiving credit for their work prefer to work alone whereas those who work in groups have diverse motives—to discover new ideas, to develop friendships, or to prove to themselves that they are superior. For some, these motives are quite stable whereas others change their orientations by the week, by the day, or even by the hour.

To provoke more discussion, Candace asks whether group work should be abolished. Instead of answering her query, students launch into a discussion of moods, their own and those of their classmates.

"I come in the class and I say to myself 'I know I can work.' And when I put my brain to saying, 'I'm gonna work,' then I'm gonna work," begins Jamika.

"When I get in, in the morning, I get crabby and I get tired. But, usually in the afternoon is when I get my best work done," admits Gary.

"Sometimes," says Latoya, "when I come in the classroom, and I see somebody I want to work with, and I ask them can I work with them, . . . If they say no, I go ask somebody else. And, if they say yes, I work with them."

"I usually look for someone who is in a good mood and if I'm in a good mood, I choose them. But if I'm in a bad mood, I usually work by myself because I don't upset anybody or anything," says Debbie.

Jamika, who is frequently crabby, says, "When I'm crabby in the morning, I always just work by myself because I don't want anybody else getting mad at me, or me getting mad at my own self." Though she sometimes advocates solitary work, at other times she seeks to be a good friend.

"Well," asserts Susan, "sometimes . . . people get me mad and sometimes I work better when I'm mad."

"If the person I want to work with is crabby, I'll say, 'I'm gonna work with someone else until you get your act together!'" Dionne scolds.

"Sometimes when some people come in, they take it out on other people and it just makes me mad," adds Deetra. "And I just get mad at other people, and that's how the day is bad."

"Sometimes . . . I work by myself because sometimes I can't find nobody else to work with," says Tyra, hinting that some days everyone is crabby.

"Sometimes when I'm mad," suggests Latoya, "I go sit and read until I calm down, or I go write poems."

Moods—their own and others'—seem a primary concern when students decide whether to collaborate and with whom. Students' sensitivity to others' perspectives, including their moods, probably contributes to the atmosphere of tolerance in this room. In this discussion, however, students simply assert their opinions and are not usually very responsive to one another's comments.[3] They can say what bothers them about their own and others' behavior, but talk about leaving the situation when someone says or does something offensive.

Tolerance is also apparent outside of class. At lunch, students are not divided by race or gender as in many integrated urban schools. European-American students, for example, can be seen learning from their African-American friends how to speak "Black English" correctly. Group membership seems to be determined by common interests, but these are not fixed.

We knew that Candace's students respected one another enough to collaborate effectively. Yet we felt the "live and let live" atmosphere could be improved on, especially so as to prevent the isolation of individuals. We agreed with Dewey (1940), who asserted that "everything which bars freedom and fullness of communication sets up barriers that divide [our community] into sets and cliques, into antagonistic sects and fractions, and thereby undermines the democratic way of life" (p. 225). There was potential for "sets and cliques" to emerge as the year progressed and we feared that this might undermine democratic participation.

We were thinking of two forms of democratic participation. In one, the goal is to obtain consensus whereas in the other the majority view is the adopted view. Candace and I agreed more with the organizers of Just Community programs, who seek group consensus (e.g., Power, Higgins, & Kohlberg, 1989). We saw the idea of majority rule as less compatible with our idea of establishing an inclusive community of scholars. So we introduced the idea of assigned groups and asked each group to create a single report, hoping that this would improve students' responsiveness toward one another. Candace concluded the discussion about collaboration by raising these possibilities for the next reports on animals. The students were excited about these ideas and became curious about how the changes would work. Over the next few days, Debbie, Jamika, Lavar, and others barraged Candace with questions in anticipation of this new arrangement.

MAKING THE CHANGE

October 15. Candace reminds the group of their previous conversation about collaboration and then introduces the new deal. Excitement mounts. As Candace announces the groups, both cheers and angry sighs arise.

"Candace! I'm the only boy in the group," whines Emmet. The girls he is assigned to work with also grumble.

"Emmet was not in this class last year," says Candace. "He needs your help to figure out how to do these groups—how to do books like this. If you look around at the groups, Jamika, there are no kids together who are used to working together."

As groups form, Candace must encourage students and repeat her instructions to select a leader and an animal name for the group. Emotion is high and students are not listening well. The calm hum of previous weeks is quickly replaced with tension and eruptions. The five groups display unique chemistries.

Jamika's Brood

Most of Jamika's classmates are entranced by her energy, self-assurance, and knack for speaking her mind eloquently. Today, however, she is crabby. "Why do I gotta work with these babies?" she grumbles to herself. "I don't wanna work with nobody. They're just a bunch of fourth-graders, she can't make me work with them!"

Dismayed as she departs to work alone, the group seeks Candace's advice. "Can we do it by ourselves?" asks Emmet. His worried look and tone of voice suggest that he has already conceded the loss.

"That's for your group to decide," says Candace, but her tone says that they should try to cooperate.

Emmet, Monique, and Karen follow Jamika around the room like ducklings, eager to please their unhappy but unanimously appointed leader. Jamika barks out orders and her entourage struggles to comply with her sketchy commands. The first assignment is to cut the paper strips necessary for writing their soon-to-be-discovered ideas.

"You go sit down. I got to get a book," Jamika orders.

When she returns, her pupils have cut the necessary slips of paper and await further instructions. Within seconds they are all working diligently, reading information from the books they have been given and writing. They ask one another about spelling and punctuation rules, but their conversation is almost imperceptible. The nickname "task master" that Candace and I privately use to describe Jamika seems apt.

Male Dominance

DeAndre is the only boy in another group of girls. "They're trying to trade me into another group!" he cries to Candace. He wants neither to be in this group, nor to be rejected.

"No trading!" Candace declares, surprised at the girls' ingenuity.

DeAndre returns shortly with a ploy. "Candace! They're climbing on the table. I don't want to work with them." Candace sends him back to try to get along for 15 minutes.

"DeAndre is supposed to do some. He needs practice working with us. That's why Candace put us in these groups," says Dionne, the group's chosen leader. More advanced into puberty, Dionne's maternal tone matches her size. "All girls and one DeAndre," she says good-naturedly.

Looking through books, the girls turn their backs on DeAndre as he walks around the table, but he will not be ignored. He struts up to each group member and threatens to beat them up if they will not accept him as leader. Relaxed, Dionne gives up her role easily.

"First we're going to do reptiles," orders DeAndre. "Then we're going to have a one-page introduction. Then a one-page report on snakes . . ."

"What about the work we already did?"

"So!"

"So, it's not about reptiles!"

DeAndre ignores this complaint and repeats, "There will be three paragraphs about snakes. One is inside the snake. Then, the outside of the snake. Then . . ."

"Why don't we each do different things?" Dionne attempts to teach DeAndre about leadership.

"Have each person do one thing," Susan agrees.

"Who's going to do inside?" continues DeAndre.

"Me!" Dionne accepts DeAndre's authority.

Sheloanda and Tyra complain that the work they've started will not be included.

"Shut up so the boy can talk," snaps Dionne.

"You do inside," says DeAndre. "Who's doing outside?"

"You can't use any of our note cards," grumbles Sheloanda.

Susan begins, "DeAndre we did these [slips about mammals]. You can do . . ."

"Pick the one you want," interrupts DeAndre. "You can do the mongrel, viper, and cobra."

"Cobra! But we don't got no books on cobras. We could do a rattlesnake," says Dionne.

Everyone starts talking. Dionne and Susan obey DeAndre. Tyra and Sheloanda defiantly resist and assail Dionne and Susan for following his orders.

"Everybody, DeAndre is the leader, do what he says," commands Dionne.

"Yeah do what I say or I'll *hit* you!" DeAndre says fiercely. "Now are we doing vipers?" DeAndre launches into his instructions.

Tyra teases, "DeAndre, you the leader. You gotta do it [the work]. You're the leader."

"I don't understand you DeAndre. Try again. You have to give us directions we can understand," says Dionne, again attempting to coach him.

With a tone of exasperation, DeAndre repeats his directions more concretely, "On half a page you write something on the inside of the snake. Write just a plain introduction on the types of snakes, where most snakes live, what they eat, you know. Listen, we're going to do five reports on five snakes! Pencils down!"

There is no reaction from the others, who are busily writing about the animals they had previously chosen. DeAndre paces around the table ordering, "Listen!" but the girls ignore him.

"Pencils down. I said down!" shouts DeAndre. "We're gonna have five reports on five snakes. You get to pick what snakes you're gonna do." Eventually, DeAndre bullies everyone into doing some sort of work about snakes.

A Leader Is Born

Lying on the floor, members of a third group examine small slips of paper.

"Pick an animal name."

They laugh and tease one another. Candace approaches and asks if they have an animal name and a leader yet.

"We're nominating!" Each person writes his or her name to be nominated as leader, producing a stalemate. They try again, but the same thing happens.

"Wait, we need two nominations!"

"How about everyone puts their names in and we pick one." They do this, and Lavar, the least popular member of the group, is selected.

"Oh!" says Lavar, stunned. He can hardly believe it.

"Yuck!" says Angela.

"Not Lavar," moans Maria.

But Christopher says, "You're leader, what do we research first, leader? OK leader, what do we do next?"

Lavar looks nervous and hurt. He gets up, paces around the room, steps into the hallway, and returns. He repeats this five times. Each time he returns, Christopher asks, directing this to the others as much as to Lavar, "What do we research first, leader?"

Jim, from another group, appears and says to Lavar, "Mathew doesn't like you." Mathew, in Jim's group, is quiet, assured, popular, and academically able.

Lavar paces the room again. Christopher asks the others, "Lavar is the leader. Do you agree?" Reluctantly all agree and by the time Lavar returns, the group is chattering happily.

"Leader, what do we do first?"

"Let's do reptiles," Maria suggests.

"No, he'll pick one and we say if we like it or not," says Christopher, emphasizing Lavar's responsibilities. He repeatedly uses the word leader and hints that Lavar must make all decisions and please the group. Christopher seems to be putting pressure on Lavar, but the group does not support this.

Wringing his hands and pulling his short hair, Lavar gets up and walks around nervously, but returns. He approaches Candace and gets encouragement, but no specific ideas.

"We're going to get in trouble!" worries Jennifer.

"Where's our leader?" Maria complains.

Lavar returns with more confidence. He asks what the group wants to study. Two children from other groups come to ask who is the leader. When they are told it is Lavar, they express disbelief and disgust.

"We're going to get in trouble." Jennifer tries to make progress.

"You pick one and we'll say if we like it," Christopher commands.

"What do you want to do first?" Lavar asks.

"No. You're the leader, you pick," others chant.

Lavar finally asks, "How about cobras?"

"No!" the group chants.

Lavar then suggests a list of aggressive or scary animals, none of which are mammals. The three girls want to study mammals, but do not say so. They simply reject Lavar's suggestions. Christopher attacks.

"You can't be our leader cause you don't pick fair choices! Let's go over there and see what they got." He checks his friend Jim's group and is consoled by the fact that they, on the verge of a fight, are worse off than he.

Lavar brings a pile of cards with pictures of animals, "Let's see what's in these cards."

Looking at each card the whole group votes no for each one. Eventually they decide to divide up the animal kingdom into major groups with some working on mammals, others reptiles, and others birds. These decisions lead to further bickering about who will work on which topic. They begin to find books and write notes, but the communal flavor has disappeared.

Lavar snaps, "What is you doin'?"

"Kangaroo," says Angela.

"I'm doing mammals!" flashes Lavar.

As Candace approaches, Lavar points to Angela and Jennifer, complaining, "They want to do mammals, they gotta do reptiles."

"I wanna do mammals," says Angela.

"How are you going to work this out?" Candace asks.

Lavar takes charge. "We gotta get this done. Come on, we gotta stop playing around! What do you want to do? Birds?" With that, the group returns to work, but all happily pursue their own interests.

A Coup

"I think Mathew should be our leader," suggests Jim.

"OK," says Deetra.

"Yeah, that's good," replies Latoya. Everyone but Debbie agrees. She pouts.

"Now you guys," continues Jim, "I don't know if you can do bones, but there are two zoo books on bones."

"Sure." "OK."

Jim leaves, approaches his friend Christopher in Lavar's group and says with delight, "They do everything I want to do! First, I say Mathew should be group leader. They say yes! Then I say, 'Let's start with badgers!' They say yes! Then I say, 'Let's start with cardinals.' They say yes! I can't believe it!"

Meanwhile, Mathew suggests, "I think we should do cardinals."

"Well, I want to do woodpeckers," says Debbie, getting snotty.

"We could each do one," compromises Mathew.

"No, everyone should do the same and it should be woodpeckers," contradicts Debbie.

Mathew and the others ignore her. "I can't wait till Thursday," says Debbie making up a due date. "This is due Thursday and I won't have to be in this stupid group."

Mathew and the others continue, ignoring Debbie. She attacks again, "Mathew, don't you know that LA Gear is out of style? Why do you wear such nerdy stuff?" (Mathew is usually more cleanly dressed than many of his classmates. He rarely wears wornout clothes—as do many of the others, including Debbie.)

Others join in. As Jim returns, Mathew leaves, crying. The others are surprised and follow him.

"We're just messing with you!" teases Debbie.

"We were just playing," consoles Deetra.

"He doesn't think you're messing with him," says Jim.

Mathew retreats to his seat, hiding his face in his hands. The group follows.

Debbie's thrill at ousting Mathew from leadership cannot be concealed by her pleas to Candace for mercy. Candace chastises Debbie for her cruelty and reminds the group of their task. They begin again. Their election for a new leader is a tie.

"We have to do everybody's vote."

"Mine isn't in it," admits dejected Mathew.

Latoya tries to coax him, "It's between you two [Deetra and Jim]. Mathew, you'll make the winning vote."

"It's between me and Deetra," interrupts Debbie. "Who wants me?"

"HUH UN!" objects Jim.

"Who wants Debbie?" chimes Latoya.

"It's between Deetra and Debbie? What about me?" cries Jim.

The group proceeds to fight about possible leaders. After about 5 minutes, Jim suddenly takes charge, "Everybody has to do five slips."

"I don't want to be in this stupid group!" whines Debbie.

"Who's going to be the writer?" says Latoya, who likes to avoid writing whenever possible.

"Everybody has to write five slips or better no matter what!" commands Jim.

After a bit more bickering, they angrily invent their own tasks. In the resulting chaos, Jim says, "Debbie, don't talk. We have to get some work done!"

"Shut up!" Debbie responds.

"Debbie quit laughing!" commands Jim, but Debbie disrupts everyone, poking fun at their handwriting, and whatever strikes her attention. She moves around the table toward Mathew. "Debbie, you sit in that corner for five minutes!" Jim orders.

"Did I start anything?" she whines, but goes to the corner anyway. From the corner, Debbie denigrates the others.

"Debbie, I'm warning you!" declares Jim. "You will sit there for two minutes and I don't want to hear another word from you! I'm serious. I'm not fooling around!"

Candace has been watching from across the room as Mathew shuts out the world with his hands and studies the table top. She turns to the one collaborating group in the room and asks Chantal and Bernadette, both quiet and serious, to invite Mathew into their group.

Chantal quietly approaches him. "Do you want to be in another group?"

"Mathew, do you want to be in this group?" adds Bernadette, pointing to her group.

His hands still over his face, Mathew angrily says, "No."

"Do you want to come and work with us?" Chantal persists gently.

Mathew lifts his face and looks at Candace. "Did Candace say?"

Bernadette leads Mathew to the sanctuary of the new group, and he explains how mean his group has been. He happily settles into this warm, sympathetic group.

Chantal, then, angrily approaches the members of his original group. "Mathew is now in *our* group," she states and lectures them on the need for an apology.

A few minutes later, Jim meets his friend Christopher at the supply cabinet.

Christopher asks, "You got a good group?" and Jim answers sadly, "No . . ."

"Too bad," his friend sympathizes.

At the end of a half hour, Candace asks them to stop, compliments them on how long they were able to work together, and asks them to come to a group meeting. Much to our surprise, the students declare the new method fun, saying that they would learn a lot and that they would do good reports. The only conflict involves Debbie and Mathew. Debbie accuses Mathew of being overly sensitive and Mathew accuses her of being mean and "despicable!" Otherwise, students say they would be happy working in these groups for the next three weeks and seem oblivious to the considerable conflict and limited progress on their reports.

CHAOS CONTINUES

That day, Candace and I tried to accept the students' positive evaluations of their assigned groups and consoled ourselves by discussing the positive developments. Lavar, who would never have been appointed leader, was clearly gaining strength. New friendships also emerged. Like adults, we concluded, children need time to adapt to new group arrangements. But our optimism faded. Throughout the next three weeks, bickering and attempts to break away from the assigned groups increased. Power had rarely been a motive in the class. Now it was a constant issue, with the balance of power changing daily.

Jamika and Emmet began to fight, causing their group to disintegrate. One afternoon, Jamika got so angry with Emmet that she stormed out of school in the middle of the day, walked the bus route home, and stayed away for two days. When she returned, ready to work again, her group members were so fearful of her temper that they asked to be assigned to other groups. Another group also disintegrated: Chantal and Bernadette worked together, closing out the rest of their group, who managed to look busy while doing almost no research. Mathew and Susan were so frustrated with their respective groups that each completed two projects: personal projects on which they lavished care and thought, and the required group projects on which their efforts were perfunctory. Of the children this new arrangement was especially intended to assist, only Sharmon, who got more help than usual, showed marked improvement. Debbie became more domineering, DeAndre more aggressive, and Sheloanda still managed to avoid most of her schoolwork.

On the day of the deadline, only a few groups had completed any sort of a report and after an additional week of encouragement from Candace, seven students still had nothing to show. DeAndre's group had done so little that they spent one afternoon, shortly after the deadline, drawing pictures to accumulate enough for a book. Everyone could talk about some new things they had learned. The reports, however, reflected their new concerns with power and credit. Students systematically put their names on each of their contributions to the group project. Most reports, furthermore, lacked elements that suggest pride. Title pages, inventive puzzles, reasons for learning about animals, author biographies, and other personal touches were rare. Writing quality also declined. Paragraphs more often consisted of disconnected sentences (e.g., "Mammals have warm blood. A fox eats field mice."), spelling was unusually poor, and many sections of the reports contained only single lines of text.

BACK TO OUR BASICS

The next reports were on evolution. Instead of gradually incorporating more aspects of the various cooperative learning models, we thought about returning to the old ways. Candace consulted with her students, and they agreed that spontaneous collaboration was better, so they went back to completing individual reports and choosing their own collaborators.

We figured that by assigning students to groups, we inadvertently put excessive restraints on the spontaneous creativity and communication of ideas that normally dominated Candace's classroom–undermining an important way in which this community of scholars helped one another learn. We made it more difficult for good ideas to spread slowly throughout the class because students were less free to approach nongroup members who might otherwise help them. Application of the metaphor of football team spirit, used by some cooperative learning theorists (e.g., Johnson & Johnson, 1975; Slavin, 1983, 1991b), led these students to restrict their thinking to match that of their group members or to quit doing tasks when their views did not conform.

All this was confirmed once students were free to choose when and with whom to collaborate. The bickering ceased. A calm hum again filled the room, and attention turned back to the substance of the reports. Students regularly changed collaborators and ideas were shared widely. It was no longer necessary to repeatedly announce upcoming deadlines and procedures for getting books and materials, or to negotiate strategies for working out interpersonal conflicts.

Most of the class also did better on their evolution reports than they did on their animal projects. The number of pages was not significantly different across the two reports. However, students wrote more on each page, included more ideas, made more illustrations, and included more elements suggesting pride in their reports (e.g., title pages, reasons why the topic was interesting). The quality of writing was also better. Sentences were more often combined into meaningful paragraphs, and students wrote to convey themes rather than single lines and disconnected thoughts. They also took time to correct their spelling, appropriately punctuate their work, and rewrite pages that were difficult to read. For Candace and me, reading the reports was once again fun.

CONSENSUS OR COMMUNICATED EXPERIENCE?

Although our attempt to gradually incorporate aspects of cooperative learning theory into Candace's room was a dismal failure, the experience proved quite fruitful in other ways. By provoking students to reflect on and discuss the fairness and effectiveness of practices intended to help them learn and the ways in which they collaborate, we learned some things we did not expect.

During the weeks when students studied evolution, Candace left an audiotape recorder in a quiet corner of the room and encouraged students to tape their discussions of these matters when they felt inclined. Students enjoyed these sessions, but in moments of passion broke a couple recorders and, on other occasions, failed to press the correct buttons. Still, some interesting fragments survived.

Angela and Latoya, for example, were having difficulty collaborating and "discussed" their problem with the recorder running. Angela thought that Latoya had not been doing her share. Here, she challenges Latoya, and Latoya explains her actions.

"[When collaborating] the person has to see that it's OK to work with that person," says Angela. "I usually pick the right people. . . . I picked a new partner [Latoya] now, and she's *not* working very nicely, but I'm getting her good. Before she was not working very good, but I've gotten her on the horsey and now we're taking a ride!"

Latoya responds to this apparent criticism cheerfully, "If you are stuck on something, and you're working with somebody, the person that knows it may help you with it. Like my friend [Angela], she helps me with a lot of stuff, and I think it's really nice for her to do that."

"Thank you, Latoya," says Angela with an audible sigh of relief. "I think I have been helping her a lot, too. But I think the most thing she has been helping me about is being my friend." In accepting Latoya's explanation, Angela seems to have come to value friendship in itself.

These girls came away from a difficult conflict with a deeper understanding of one another. By discussing what makes a good collaborator, they resolved their differences in a way that was not personally threatening to either of them. Their subtlety and honesty are impressive, but more importantly they worked through their conflict rather than avoiding it by choosing another collaborator. They also managed to achieve consensus.

Nevertheless, the project as a whole and some recorded conversations provoked us to recognize problems with trying to obtain consensus. We came to recognize what Dewey (1940) meant when he said:

> Democracy as a way of life is controlled by personal faith in personal day-by-day working together with others. Democracy is the belief that even when the needs and ends or consequences are different for each individual, the habit of amicable co-operation—which may include, as in sport, rivalry and competition—is itself a priceless addition to life. To take as far as possible every conflict which arises—and they are bound to arise—out of the

atmosphere and medium of force, of violence as a means of settlement, into that of discussion and of intelligence, is to treat those who disagree— even profoundly—with us as those from whom we may learn, and in so far, as friends. (pp. 225–226)

Perhaps the essence of democracy lies in the ability to sustain conversation with those who disagree with us. In the following example, Candace's students teach us how they can learn even from those with whom they profoundly disagree.

Jamika, the girl who left school over an argument with Emmet, is temporarily kicked out of her friendship group for a transgression known, at this point, only to her friends. In the initial class discussion on selecting collaborators she said, "When you do the report [by yourself] you feel good about yourself and *you're* the one that's getting the credit." Her actions throughout the year, particularly during the experiment, appear to confirm the impression that she values solitary work. Yet the following discussion suggests that Jamika's position may be more complex. In order to collaborate, she appears to require intimate friendship and trust, but is fearful that her friends will betray her.

Today she is lonely and talks with Latoya and Angela, classmates she would normally shun. She struggles to learn how these girls, who change collaborators often, manage to cope with the fear of betrayal. The girls express their differences and struggle to learn from one another, but do not expect to attain consensus.

"Latoya, when you working on the report, who do you choose to work with?"

"I will choose someone that is like in the fourth or fifth grade and someone who works really, really nice."

"What if you think that person is gonna work really, really nice and they don't? What'll you do?" Jamika queries.

"I will at least stop working with them and go somewhere else and find someone else to work with." This line of questioning continues with Jamika trying, without success, to help Latoya see the importance of trust. She eventually gets frustrated and turns to Angela.

"Angela, when you working with people, how do you choose? How do you know that they gonna work good?"

"Well, I don't really know how they're gonna work unless they're already started. And if they're not working right, then I just leave and go with somebody else that will work right."

"But what if they *say* they gonna work good. Whatever [they do], they say they are gonna work good. What do you do?" challenges Jamika.

"Well, I just give it another try or something. And I'll see if they're gonna work good, and I'll try to pull them together. And if I do, then that's how it works."

Jamika continues to needle Angela about the issue of trust and friendship, but Angela doesn't seem to grasp her intent. Jamika sighs heavily. Angela, perhaps picking up on her frustration, asks, "Jamika, when you come to school, what do you look for in a person?"

"Well, sometimes when I choose people that I work with in a report— sometimes I already know who I'm gonna work with because the people that I work with, I mostly all the time work with." These are the members of Jamika's friendship group.

Angela, excluded from that group, has had her feelings hurt by their exclusive attitudes more than once. She needles Jamika with, "What if, [as she now is,] you are mad at that person who you want to work with?"

"Well, then sometimes if I'm mad at the person . . . if I got them mad at me, I would apologize. But if they got mad at me for no reason, I'd just work with [another friend]."

"How do you choose your friends to work with?" prods Angela.

"What do you mean how do I choose them?" Jamika takes her friends so for granted that she seems not to have thought of ways to make new ones.

"Like if they're working fine would you pick 'em or not? If somebody's working very, very good, and you don't like them . . . if they are working very, very good and everybody else is working very, very bad, why or why not would you pick that person?"

"Sometimes I don't work with people. . . . Say like if the teacher put us in a group and I don't like that person. I don't think I would work because I don't feel comfortable sitting in a group doing reports with people that I don't like. But then, sometimes if they not getting on my nerves and being a real pain in the neck, I would sometimes give them a chance . . ."

Backed into a corner, Jamika tries to explain why she has broken her friendship rule to collaborate with Latoya and Angela, girls she would normally reject. This discussion does not end with a clear statement about the role of trust in collaboration, but the girls took the issue as far as they were able at the time. They discussed their concerns and explored ways in which they often miscommunicate. Like many discussions, this one ends neither with the mere agreement to disagree, nor with consensus. Each participant addressed her own agenda, but sought to learn more about herself and others through negotiation.

NOW WHAT DO THE CUSTOMERS THINK?

December 14. At a class meeting the day the projects were handed in, Candace asked, "I'm really curious, and so is Terri, about why this project was so much better than the last one. Last time I had to get on your case every day to get to work and [constantly] remind you of the deadlines. This time you worked together so well, and you all got your projects done on time. What was the difference? How did you choose your groups? How did you decide whether to work in groups or work alone?"

"I didn't join a group because when you're by yourself, you can decide how much you want to do and when," interrupts Debbie.

"I noticed a difference," Candace continues. "For me it was a lot easier. Your ideas were better. Why did this happen? Why did some of you work in groups and why did some of you work alone?"

"I choose my friends that work good together," begins Jim, eagerly. "I like that. I like it when we choose our own groups because you get put with people that work good, friends that work good, and not with others. I like working with friends, not because they are friends, but because they *work good* together."

"It seems like you get more done," adds Mathew. "You get more work."

"The group helps you stay on task."

Students repeat the now familiar themes of hard work and laziness.[4]

"What happens when you play around?" asks Candace, encouraging students to elaborate on their theme of effort. "Emmet, how about you? Why did you switch groups?" Emmet thinks, but Dionne speaks.

"I wanted to work with different people."

"So you don't really think about it? You just float around?"

"Not really," says Emmet, slowly.

"Why do you choose the people you do?"

"It feels more *comfortable*," responds Dionne, who, during the experiment, maintained harmony with DeAndre by giving up her position as leader. She regularly helps classmates find collaborators and resolve conflicts, yet never asserts a formula for making such decisions.

"It feels more comfortable working with friends. It feels uncomfortable with other people," adds Susan.

"We're getting better and better at reports," says Jim, pleased with himself.

"Why are you getting better?" prods Candace.

"I didn't have a real good group before," responds Jim.

"I took some home."

"Why?"

"I thought if I did a really good report, I'd *feel better* than I did last time."

"When we got going it was fun and we really got into it," says Dionne.

Students continued asserting these same themes. They would not or could not elaborate on specific things that could help them feel "comfortable" or "better." Candace moves on, "I'm really interested to know why that happened. If you think of any other reasons, I hope you will tell me. The next report after the holidays will be on Native Americans. What should I do about groups? Should I assign groups?"

"NO!" the class unanimously shouts.

"Should I make each one of you do your reports by yourself?" challenges Candace. Again there is a chorus of no, but Jamika and Debbie loudly call, "Yes!"

"Should I have all of you find your own groups to work in?" Most students say yes, but those who prefer to work by themselves say no.

"How about if I let you choose to work in groups or to do your own reports?"

Their yes is unanimous.

For Candace, the role of teacher did not involve finding the "right" practice to apply to all situations. Our changes, of course, reminded her of that, and she found herself renewing her respect for the personal and particular ways of her students. She always spent a lot of time thinking through the implications of what she did and said, and let her students establish conduct rules, set up procedures for disciplinary action, and plan extracurricular activities. Now, she also overtly encourages students to express their reasons for learning and to negotiate the ways in which they might do so. She does not passively stand by and let her students "do their own thing," or coerce them into one way. She knows that her job is to help students clarify their own purposes. To do that she must help each student find a personal key. This search is no solitary activity: It requires others with whom to respectfully disagree.

REMEMBERING TO LISTEN

We had not really understood what the children told us about how they choose collaborators before we assigned them to groups. Had we understood the importance of trust, friendship, and mood to these children, we might never have assigned groups. The children told us that they came to school with diverse priorities, but we had not fully heard them. No wonder power plays became so prevalent.

Cooperative learning models operate as if these priorities will not influence students' approach to assigned tasks, but Candace's students told us that they could not achieve their purposes and learn the same way. Some students, like Jamika and Gary, insisted on defining school as a test. They emphasized the need for solitary work and worried about getting credit for their accomplishments. Others, like Debbie and DeAndre, defined school as a contest. They asserted their superiority over others and mocked those who did not measure up to their standards. Furthermore, there were students who emphasized learning and intellectual risk-taking. Like Mathew and Latoya, they were quick to ask for help from their peers and were not embarrassed by their mistakes. There were also people like Chantal and Monique, who valued friendship in its own right and sought to sustain community as an end in itself.

Researchers who are concerned with describing typical or average motives and prescribing general policies or classroom practices would never uncover the things Candace learns about her students' motivation. They spend their time designing practices that reflect their own particular visions of cooperative learning and argue about the superiority of these practices. In doing so, they join a conversation or debate with other researchers about how education should be conducted. In these discussions, the convictions of individual researchers are never met with universal agreement. Overall, the academic community tolerates diverse priorities or visions of what schools should accomplish. Ironically, however, the individual members of this community rarely advocate that such tolerance be accorded to students. Each prophet argues that his or her vision of truth applies to all children.

Disastrous though our attempts to improve responsiveness were in some respects, they did alert everyone to the value of discussing reasons for our actions. The children showed us that they can listen, argue, and change their priorities. We learned that finding the right way to collaborate will forever remain a controversial moral task. Our community of scholars came, in other words, to agree with W. V. Quine (1987), who wrote,

> Some restraints on democratic tolerance are vital to the survival of democracy. Excessive restraints, on the other hand, would be an abdication of democracy. Such, then, is the delicate balance of tolerance. All of us, governors and governed, appreciate the weighty considerations on both sides of the balance. I am not one of those, if such there be, who knows how to best strike the balance. I can only appreciate the delicacy. (pp. 206–207)

Yet to "treat those who disagree—even profoundly—with us as those from whom we may learn, and in so far, as friends" (Dewey, 1940, p. 226) we require more than tolerance. Individuals have to relish and respond to one another's differences. As Dewey asserts:

> To co-operate by giving differences a chance to show themselves because of the belief that the expression of difference is not only a right of the other persons but is a means of enriching one's own life-experience, is inherent in the democratic personal way of life. (p. 226)

Acknowledgment. The assistance of William Ayers, Fran Blumberg, and David Hansen on earlier drafts of this paper is greatly appreciated, as is the editorial assistance of Susan Nolen and Algis Sodonis. Our thanks also to John Schmuhl, principal of MacDowell Elementary School.

NOTES

1. Candace's students are unusual in that they have been collaborating since preschool. MacDowell is a public Montessori school in which there is an explicit attempt to help children develop positive social relationships. The Montessori program attempts to teach children to respect one another and to build a collective, communal order while becoming autonomous learners (Montessori, 1965).

2. Although the use of "bribes" and "group grade grubbing" is believed to undermine intrinsic interest in learning (Kohn, 1991), some cooperative learning theorists claim that it is essential if students are to continue collaborating (Johnson & Johnson, 1975; Slavin, 1991a). Others have no definitive position on this, but suggest that extrinsic rewards might enhance student motivation (Sharan et al., 1984).

3. Blum (1987) defines responsiveness as a moral phenomenon that encompasses the interaction of both cognitive and affective dimensions. Responsiveness is not a purely rational willing of another person's good: It involves taking action to address another's condition. Merely understanding another's condition is not sufficient for responsiveness since this understanding can be used to manipulate or to ridicule. Furthermore, experiencing the same feeling as the other person is neither necessary nor sufficient for responsiveness: A person can be truly concerned about another's pain without experiencing the same feelings of pain or distress.

4. Ability is not a central concern in any of the conversations I observed. The preoccupation with effort common among Candace's students' would be predicted from Piagetian-style interviews, conducted by Nicholls and his colleagues, on children's conceptions of ability and effort (Nicholls, 1989). These studies suggest that most fourth- and fifth-graders are more likely to believe, as the class discussions imply, that if everyone applies equal effort, they will achieve equally.

REFERENCES

Blum, L. (1987). Particularity and responsiveness. In J. Kagan & S. Lamb (Eds.), *The emergence of morality in young children* (pp. 306-337). Chicago: University of Chicago Press.

Bowles, S., & Gintis, H. (1976). *Schooling in capitalist America: Educational reform and the contradictions of economic life*. New York: Basic Books.

Dewey, J. (1940). Creative democracy—The task before us. In *The philosopher of the common man: Essays in honor of John Dewey to celebrate his eightieth birthday* (pp. 220-228). New York: G. P. Putnam's Sons.

Dewey, J. (1944). *Democracy and education*. New York: The Free Press. (Original work published 1916)

Johnson, D. W., & Johnson, R. T. (1975). *Learning together and alone: Cooperation, competition and individualization*. Englewood Cliffs, NJ: Prentice Hall.

Johnson, D. W., & Johnson, R. T. (1989). *Cooperation and competition: Theory and research*. Edina, MN: Interaction Book Company.

Kohn, A. (1991). Group grade grubbing versus cooperative learning. *Educational Leadership*, *48*, 83-87.

Lepper, M. R., & Greene, D. (Eds.). (1978). *The hidden costs of reward: New perspectives on the psychology of human motivation*. Hillsdale, NJ: Erlbaum.

Montessori, M. (1965). *The Montessori method*. New York: Schocken Books.

Nicholls, J. G. (1989). *The competitive ethos and democratic education*. Cambridge: Harvard University Press.

Power, F. C., Higgins, A., & Kohlberg, L. (1989). *Lawrence Kohlberg's approach to moral education*. New York: Columbia University Press.

Quine, W. V. (1987). *Quiddities: An intermittently philosophical dictionary*. Cambridge: Harvard University Press.

Sharan, S. (1980). Cooperative learning in small groups: Recent methods and effects on achievement, attitudes, and ethnic relations. *Review of Educational Research*, *50*, 241-271.

Sharan, S., Kussel, P., Hertz-Lazarowitz, R., Bejarano, Y., Raviv, S., & Sharan, Y. (1984). *Cooperative learning in the classroom: Research in desegregated schools*. Hillsdale, NJ: Erlbaum.

Slavin, R. E. (1983). *Cooperative learning*. New York: Longman.

Slavin, R. E., (1991a). Synthesis of research on cooperative learning. *Educational Leadership*, *48*, 71-82.

Slavin, R. E. (1991b). Group rewards make groupwork work: Response to Kohn. *Educational Leadership*, *48*, 89-91.

Conclusion
THREATS TO CREATIVITY AND COMMUNITY
John G. Nicholls

We have argued that abstract generalizations should not be seen as the ultimate or most important form of knowledge about student motivation and education. Yet we have tacitly advanced a generalization. Namely, as Deborah Meier (1991) puts it,

> A good school is always particular. . . . Its particularity grows out of the fact that the school is the hard-won and carefully crafted creation of a particular group of people . . . who know one another well and take one another seriously (which involves quarreling). (pp. 339–340)

Students should be included in these negotiations or quarrels, which are about what a good school is as much as about how to get one. They should be included not merely because this will increase their motivation or make them learn more effectively the lessons others have assigned them. They should be included because the intelligent, collaborative formation of the purposes that govern action is the essence of freedom and of democratic social life.

Many beginning teachers set out hopefully, thinking that students are waiting to be liberated. Ira Shor (1986) encourages this view when he writes that

> students will resist any process that disempowers them. . . . teacher-talk, passive instruction in pre-set materials, punitive testing, moronic back-to-basics and mechanical drills . . . the exclusion of student co-participation in curriculum design and governance. (p. 183)

But students often will participate in their own disempowerment. Like Lakita, in Cathryn Busch's chapter, they will resist the idea that they should participate in curriculum design and governance. And students can both want and oppose freedom. In Susan Hazzard's second-grade class, Peter was one of the livelier contributors to classroom negotiations.

Yet he also complained, "There's so much work and you're always doing conversations and I'm not learning anything. In kindergarten I got information like a computer would. . . . I knew all I had to know for first and second grade in kindergarten. It's conversation, conversation, and we hardly get anything accomplished" (Nicholls & Hazzard, 1993, p. 172). Sue's favored method for dealing with conflict is respectful conversation. When Peter's contribution to the conversation is "It's conversation, conversation, and we hardly get anything accomplished," he presents Sue with a dilemma.

As James Herndon (1969) found, students often insist that learning spelling and sentences, and having a teacher who "makes" them work hard and does not encourage discussion, is "the way it's spozed to be." Linda McNeil (1986) observed high school students declaring teachers fair when they reduced complex and controversial topics like union history to lists of discrete facts to be memorized. We might find their conception of fairness distorted, but teachers are in for a shock if they presume that all children yearn to negotiate the purposes that govern their learning. Fear of freedom is real, among students. Some resonate with larger, intransigent forces from outside classrooms that would deny them and others the right to inquire about reasons for learning. Countering their values can involve countering the values of their families and alienating them from those families (Foster, 1986; Harman & Edelsky, 1989). Parents who want their children to run well in the existing academic race can, reasonably enough, see attempts to question the rules of that race appear as attempts to handicap their children. This presents a substantial dilemma.

Sylvia Ashton-Warner felt restricting forces from outside her classroom, and hid her evolving purposes in the shade behind her eyes where the inspector could not see. And this was in an earlier New Zealand where, in some respects, there was more room for teacher initiative than in current schools, especially urban ones (Weiner, 1993). Even so, Ashton-Warner avoided some of the demands many teachers of that time and place faced. She was able to shape her creative vision of teaching partly by neglecting aspects of what most would consider normal teaching duties (Hood, 1988). Not all are so lucky or so willful.

Some years before the events recorded in Chapter 6, Susan Hazzard was close to leaving teaching. One parent's complaint led the superintendent to insist that Sue follow a precisely scheduled order of work, much of which was well beyond the reach of her students. Under that regime, she could hardly have encouraged negotiation of the curriculum. Like most teachers, she still faces constraints that even second-graders can detect. Her student Dan was surprised to learn that individual teachers did not select the texts used in their classrooms: "Why," he burst out, "can't teachers teach how they want and not all the same?" (Nicholls & Hazzard, 1993, p. 100). Dan will not be pleased to learn of moves toward national standards and a national curriculum.

Candace Jordan has run a classroom that is atypical among contemporary urban schools. She can do so partly because, in her specialty school, she teaches the same students for two and three years rather than for the usual one year. This increases the chance that she and her students will become a "group of people . . . who know one another well and take one another seriously." She is also helped by the fact that her school rarely administers standardized tests and does not use workbooks, textbooks, or grades. The policies and traditions of the school help protect Candace from parental pressure for immediate gains in test scores. They assist her in hearing her students and helping them listen to one another.

Individual teachers must take as well as be allowed initiative. When Cathryn Busch, as principal, sought volunteers to try something new, she got only one. For Lee Colsant, school reform was like the 747s flying over his school and not landing. He decided to do something himself. We need to take risks, even if only in the shade behind our eyes where the inspector cannot see.

Nevertheless, we should not expect to be saved by a breed of super-teachers committed to daily triumph over school systems that are opposed to local community and initiative. Experienced teachers tell generations of student teachers that their youthful idealism is misplaced. New teachers often conform or give up. Rather than dismiss the courage and competence of every rising generation of hopefuls, we might reflect on the problems they face. (The following offer both hope and realism: Foster, 1986; Goodman, 1992; Herndon, 1969; Jervis & Montag, 1991; Nehring, 1989; Sarason, 1993; Weiner, 1993; Welsh, 1986.)

Teachers need environments that encourage them to listen to those with whom they work and to negotiate new and better ways of living and learning (Maehr & Anderman, 1993; McNeil, 1986; Sarason, 1990). We need systems that foster strong forms of civil society—local democratic practices in schools. Civil society exists when citizens act on their own initiatives, and not in response to rules made by the state (Revel, 1993). It exists when people can form their own purposes, execute those purposes, and reconstruct them in light of the consequences. It dies when purposes are determined by remote committees, administrators, or lawmakers. In many countries, civil society died under Communism. But elected officials can enact laws that destroy civil society (Barber, 1984; Revel, 1993). When regimes that destroy civil society collapse, they leave wastelands where little regenerates. "Freedom of culture does not guarantee that only masterpieces will be produced. But we do know for sure that cultural totalitarianism sterilizes talent" (Revel, 1993, p. 112).

The concern for freedom is not the particular property of the radical left—politically correct or not. In his "military industrial complex" speech of 1961, President Eisenhower warned of a coming sterilization of talent. He feared the effect on local initiative of the federal government's role in the direction of scientific inquiry.

> The prospect of domination of the nation's scholars by Federal employment, project allocations, and the power of money is ever present—and is gravely to be regarded.
> ... in holding scientific research and discovery in respect, as we should, we must also be alert to the equal and opposite danger that public policy could itself become the captive of a scientific-technological elite. (McDougall, 1985, p. 229)

At the time an observer added, "We are now coming to a time in which it is very hard to maintain private initiative and private property because so much of what we do—including science—is done by large groups or by the state itself. More and more we tend to resemble the Soviets, however much we disclaim this" (McDougall, 1985, p. 230).

Cultural totalitarianism reigns in many schools where purposes are defined by distant experts and committees and by scores on tests developed far away. Many of our schools, taking test scores as the measure of their worth, seem to have lost that essential property of living systems: the ability to renew themselves. They resemble the cultural wastelands produced by Communism (Revel, 1993). They treat reforms that might increase civil society—local initiative and community—as infectious invasions to be attacked and destroyed (Gibboney, 1994).

It is almost as if teachers worked in automobile factories at a time when Washington had decreed that only a small number of standard cars, each with precisely defined designs, would be made. Different companies would produce the same cars. Customers could choose only between versions of standard designs made by different manufacturers. This narrow vision of quality is hardly likely to inspire those in the factories to initiative and innovation.

But things are even worse for "producers" and "consumers" of education. The test scores, on which school districts, schools, teachers, and individual students are compared, do not specify anything as coherent as a car. A car, even a standardized car, can stand on its own wheels and go places. The tests, on the other hand, demand discrete skills and knowledge that, on their own, are useful mainly for passing more such tests.

The tests demand something analogous to the production of standard-ized tires, interior lights, carburetors, piston rings, and so on. A high test score does not indicate that the parts are joined into a functioning sys-tem—an evolving person devoted to work of integrity and coherence.

Worse yet, many parents, teachers, and principals—adult customers in the education market—accept high test scores as the product schools should compete to produce. They would never evaluate automobiles in this way. With a car, they pay attention to the whole: its economy, dura-bility, speed, or beauty, the ways its many parts come together. With education, they often do not. All this would be disturbing if we made cars in this fashion. It is all the more disturbing for education because, unlike cars, persons cannot be assembled by others. They can be helped and provoked, but in the end they must put themselves together, which is why the negotiation of the reasons for learning must be every student's task.

We are urged to let market forces and competition improve our schools. But when the product is standardized in advance, competition mimics the obviously defunct Soviet way of doing business—it realizes Eisenhower's worst fears. The self-contradictory Communist notion of a dictatorship of the proletariat is matched by the contemporary compe-tition, between and within schools, for high test scores. For all but a pe-culiarly robust and resourceful few, this kills creativity and community.

Teachers have to come out of their classrooms to work for condi-tions that define teaching as a constant process of moral inquiry in which students are included. They must work to ensure that national and local debates reflect more of the complexity of students' and teachers' lives in schools. They must keep open for negotiation the point of schooling—our reasons for learning (Barone, 1992; Cochran-Smith & Lyttle, 1993; Schubert & Ayres, 1992).

REFERENCES

Barber, B. (1984). *Strong democracy: Participatory democracy for a new age.* Berkeley: University of California Press.

Barone, T. E. (1992). A narrative of enhanced professionalism: Educational researchers and popular storybooks about schoolpeople. *Educational Researcher, 21*, 15–24.

Cochran-Smith, M., & Lyttle, S. L. (1993). *Inside/outside: Teacher research and knowledge.* New York: Teachers College Press.

Foster, H. L. (1986). *Ribbin', jivin', and playin' the dozens: The persistent dilemma of our schools.* New York: Herbert L. Foster Associates.

Gibboney, R. A. (1994). School reform and the tragic sense of possibility. *Current Issues in Education, 11*, 3–13.

Goodman, J. (1992). *Elementary education for critical democracy*. Albany: State University of New York Press.

Harman, S., & Edelsky, C. (1989). The risks of whole language literacy: Alienation and connection. *Language Arts, 66*, 392–405.

Herndon, J. (1969). *The way it's spozed to be*. New York: Bantam.

Hood, L. (1988). *Sylvia! A biography of Sylvia Ashton-Warner*. New York: Penguin.

Jervis, K., & Montag, C. (1991). *Progressive education for the 1990s: Transforming practice*. New York: Teachers College Press.

Maehr, M. L., & Anderman, E. M. (1993). Reinventing schools for early adolescents: Emphasizing task goals. *The Elementary School Journal, 93*, 593–610.

McDougall, W. A. (1985). *. . . the heavens and the earth: A political history of the space age*. New York: Basic Books.

McNeil, L. (1986). *Contradictions of control: School structure and school knowledge*. New York: Routledge & Kegan Paul.

Meier, D. W. (1991, September 23). The little schools that could. *The Nation*, pp. 338–340.

Nehring, J. (1989). *"Why do we gotta do this stuff Mr. Nehring?" Notes from a teacher's day in school*. New York: Fawcett.

Nicholls, J. G., & Hazzard, S. P. (1993). *Education as adventure: Lessons from the second grade*. New York: Teachers College Press.

Revel, J.-F. (1993). *Democracy against itself: The future of the democratic impulse*. New York: Free Press.

Sarason, S. B. (1990). *The predictable failure of school reform: Can we change course before it's too late?* San Francisco: Jossey-Bass.

Sarason, S. B. (1993). *You are thinking of teaching?* San Francisco: Jossey-Bass.

Schubert, W. H., & Ayres, W. C. (1992). *Teacher lore: Learning from our own experience*. White Plains, NY: Longman.

Shor, I. (1986). *Culture wars: School and society in the conservative restoration, 1969–1984*. Boston: Routledge & Kegan Paul.

Weiner, L. (1993). *Preparing teachers for urban schools: Lessons from thirty years of school reform*. New York: Teachers College Press.

Welsh, P. (1986). *Tales out of school*. New York: Penguin.

About the Editors and the Contributors

John G. Nicholls was born in New Zealand, where he obtained teacher certification from Wellington Teachers College and a Ph.D. from Victoria University of Wellington. He was a public school and university teacher in New Zealand. In the United States, he taught educational psychology at the University of Illinois at Champaign-Urbana and Purdue University and most recently taught at the University of Illinois at Chicago before his death in September 1994. His interest in developing students as educational theorists and as shapers of the curriculum lives on.

Theresa A. Thorkildsen is assistant professor of educational psychology at the University of Illinois at Chicago. She received her doctorate from Purdue University in 1988. Her research interests include the development of reasoning about social justice, students' views on fair and effective classroom practices, and moral development.

Cathryn Busch grew up in Chicago where she has worked as an elementary school teacher and principal. She received a B.A. in Elementary Education from the University of Illinois at Chicago in 1976 and a M.A. in Educational Administration and Supervision from Chicago State University in 1985. Currently she is completing her Ph.D. in Curriculum and Instruction at the University of Illinois at Chicago. Her research interest is the educational experiences of minority and low-income students.

Lee C. Colsant, Jr. began his teaching career in Quebec, Canada. He returned to the United States where, as a teaching assistant at the University of Missouri, he completed a M.A. in French. For the subsequent 19 years he has taught in the Chicago Public School System. He recently began doctoral studies in Education at the University of Illinois at Chicago. He is interested in children and in making school come alive. It is ironic that he feels he has only now begun to teach.

Susan P. Hazzard grew up in Pittsburgh. Her B.A. and M.A. degrees in education are from Purdue University. She has taught second and third grades since 1968 in West Lafayette, Indiana. She taught a process approach to science at Purdue in 1973 and has conducted various teacher workshops. Her commitment to teaching includes participation in local branches of teachers' organizations. She has especially enjoyed working with children from many nations, even though—as with the class described in this book—often three quarters of the students leave the school district in the course of three years.

Candace Jordan teaches 4th and 5th grades at MacDowell Elementary School in Milwaukee, Wisconsin. She received her Montessori training at the International Montessori Institute in Bergamo, Italy and taught at Toronto Montessori School. She has taught in Milwaukee Public Schools for 13 years and continues to look for ways to adapt the Montessori philosophy to address current problems in the education of urban children.

Susan B. Nolen obtained her teaching certificate at Lewis & Clark College in Portland, Oregon. She taught deaf students at elementary and high school levels for four years before obtaining her Ph.D. in Educational Psychology from Purdue University. She currently teaches at the University of Washington in Seattle. Her research concerns the relationship between motivation and learning in students of all ages.

Krisann Pergande has worked in Milwaukee Public Schools for 15 years. She is assistant principal at 38th Street School, which has an ungraded, open education program, and is working on her doctorate at the University of Wisconsin-Milwaukee. She has learned much by visiting schools in many countries throughout the world. Her research interests include school reform, professional development, and methods for facilitating community involvement in education.

Marue English Walizer is the Director of the Teacher Preparation Program and the Office of Special Educational Programs at Princeton University and teaches the Senior Seminar in Education there. She earned a M.A. in English at Rutgers University and her Ed.D. from the Harvard Graduate School of Education, where she also served for two years on the editorial board of the *Harvard Educational Review*. Prior to her doctoral work, she taught English for over 20 years in public high schools in Connecticut and New Jersey and was a Fulbright exchange teacher to The Netherlands. She continues to be interested in exploring the craft knowledge implicit in teachers' stories and how these convey important ideas about both teaching and learning.

Index